PERTH

DAVID WHISH-WILSON lives in Fremantle, Western
Australia, where he teaches creative writing at Curtin
University. He has written about Cathedral Square,
Cathedral Square: The historic heart of Perth, and *Perth* was
shortlisted for the WA Premier's award. He is also an
acclaimed crime writer, with his first novel *Line of Sight*
shortlisted for the 2012 Ned Kelly award. His most
recent novels are *The Coves*, *True West* and *Shore Leave*.

JOONDALUP

TRIGG

SCARBOROUGH

OSBORNE
PARK

SUBIACO

CLAREMONT
COTTESLOE

ROTTNEST
ISLAND

SWAN

Fremantle Port

Fremantle
Prison

FREMANTLE

COOLBELLU

South Fremantle
Power Station

COOGEE

ROCKINGHAM

ELLENBROOK

MIRRABOOKA

BALCATTA

MORLEY

MIDLAND

GUILDFORD

MUNDARING

MOUNT
LAWLEY

MAYLANDS

ings Park

Yagan

HEIRISSON
ISLAND

GOOSEBURY HILL

SOUTH
PERTH

BENTLEY

LESMURDIE

ER

The Old Swan Brewery

PERTH

CANNING RIVER

TADALE

ROSSMOYNE

VILLE

WILLETON

THORNLIE

RDOCH

CANNING
VALE

BULLCREEK

GOSNELLS

IBRA
AKE

JANDAKOT

ROLEYSTONE

KELMSCOTT

COCKBURN
CENTRAL

ARMADALE

MANDURAH

'*Perth* filled caverns in my knowledge of my home town. The ambience of Perth that David describes is very much how I have seen it. Particularly the light. A bright, encompassing, defining light. It is a joy to read something which so perfectly amplifies and improves your view of the world.' – The Honourable Kim Beazley, Governor of Western Australia

'a textured, nuanced portrait of a city still in the throes of growing pains' – *The West Australian*

'Whish-Wilson's chronicle is not a conventional history, but rather an impressionistic, anecdotal, and highly personal account, which, like the city it depicts, strikes a delicate balance between opposing styles. The narrative moves easily from passages of sensuous, almost lyrical prose to a more informal oral storytelling tone.' – *Australian Book Review*

'... what recommends *Perth* above all is the great generosity, inclusiveness and idiosyncrasy of its vision.' – Gail Jones, *The Canberra Times*

'Poetic and lyrical …' – Sally Webb, *The Sydney Morning Herald*

'What he has written is a book on Perth that attains at times to the status of poetry. Indeed, so rich and lyrical is *Perth*, so acute in its insights and adept in its composition, that (G K) Chesterton's paradox would appear well-founded.' – Richard King, *The Australian*

'David Whish-Wilson has written a deeply personal history, combining psychogeography, historical information, and literary citations and imaginings. His range is huge and his writing vivacious and fascinating … But what is charming about this book is how much is unexpected: A memory of his father, a Vietnam vet who played for West Perth, introduces the topic of local football; references to the bushranger Moondyne Joe lie alongside a history of Fremantle jail; sentimental attachment to the grave of Bon Scott gives the mass-cultural context of Perth's music scene in the '70s and '80s. Whish-Wilson has a shrewd eye for the quirky and the bizarre, but what recommends *Perth* above all is the great generosity, inclusiveness and idiosyncrasy of its vision.' – *The Age*

'*Perth* is a deeply personal take on the physical and cultural landscape of Perth and the "emotional landscape" that runs through and around it … it is clear that Whish-Wilson loves Perth deeply. Readers will thrill to his descriptions of its ecology and eclectic, and often controversial, architecture, as well as to the riverine quality of his prose and its gentle metaphorical undercurrents. At times, the book gives the distinct impression of having been written in a kind of reverie.' Richard King, *The Australian*

PERTH

DAVID
WHISH-WILSON

NEWSOUTH

For Ollie and Jean, Jack and Doreen,
Tony and Rosemary,
and Bella, Max, Fairlie and Luka

A NewSouth book

Published by
NewSouth Publishing
University of New South Wales Press Ltd
University of New South Wales
Sydney NSW 2052
AUSTRALIA
newsouthpublishing.com

© David Whish-Wilson 2013, 2020
First published 2013
New edition 2020

10 9 8 7 6 5 4 3 2 1

 A catalogue record for this book is available from the National Library of Australia

ISBN: 9781742237053 (paperback)
           9781742244969 (ebook)
           9781742249506 (ePDF)

Cover design Sandy Cull, gogoGingko
Internal design Josephine Pajor-Markus
Cover photo Robert Montgomery
Image on pp. xii–xiii Street art on Grand Lane, Perth
Map David Atkinson, handmademaps.com

UNSW
SYDNEY

Contents

They are always with us, the people of other eras that exist alongside our own, quietly watching the new psyche of the city take form as the world that they inhabited is redrawn, torn down, reclaimed and redeveloped. Their presence is fainter, less vociferous than it was when the city was theirs, but they shadow it, and feed into it ... There are lives and spirits and maps and boundaries that they follow which newcomers cannot see.

Stephen Kinnane, *Shadow Lines*

Introduction

It's late afternoon on a spring day, and I'm looking out over Perth as I wander alongside the floor-to-ceiling windows on the fifteenth storey of Gordon Stephenson House. This government building is new, part of the award-winning one40william project that rises over the equally new Perth Underground train station. The windows are tinted green but they're clear enough that I can see squalls running low and fumy to the south, trailing ropes of grey rain. And yet the sky above the CBD is blue, and the streets are awash with brilliant light. Even through the jade glass I can feel sunshine on my face.

I've spent the afternoon in the temporary home of the City of Perth Library, working my way through the archives. While there are as many 'Perths' as people who live here, of course, I wanted to commence the research for this book by revisiting two stories that have stayed with me over the years: one because I didn't understand its significance as a child, the other because it captured my imagination. This beginning also reflects the approach that I've taken in the following chapters. Each takes its name from a natural formation or feature of Perth – the river, the coast, the plain and the light – that has evoked characters and events, moving backwards and forwards in time. The two stories that made an impression on me as a child take place in different centuries, but both represent something about the character of the city I call home.

The first time I heard the story of Fanny Balbuk, she wasn't given a name. I can't even remember which teacher told me about her in primary school. He must have been a good storyteller, though, because the images were powerfully clear. Fanny Balbuk came from the Whadjuk clan of the Nyungar, the Indigenous people of south-west Western Australia, and one of the largest language groups in the country. She was born and raised on the Swan River at Matagarup, or Heirisson Island. The year of her birth was 1840, barely a decade after Europeans established the Swan River Colony and not long before her father died on Rottnest Island. Like many of his kinsmen, he'd been imprisoned there for stealing flour.

Balbuk expressed her frustration at the development of the Georgian village on her country by stubbornly continuing to follow the tracks of her ancestors. According to Daisy Bates, the Irish Australian who observed and recorded Western Australian Indigenous culture in the first half of the twentieth century:

> To the end of her life [Balbuk] raged and stormed
> at the usurping of her beloved home ground ...
> a straight track led to the place where once she
> had gathered jilgies and vegetable food with the
> women, in the swamp where Perth railway station
> now stands. Through fences and over them,
> Balbuk took the straight track to the end. When
> a house was built in the way, she broke its fence
> palings with her digging stick and charged up the
> steps and through the rooms.

Bates goes on to describe how one of Balbuk's 'favourite annoyances was to stand at the gates of Government House, reviling all who dwelt within, in that the stone gates guarded by a sentry enclosed her grandmother's burial ground'.

Neither Bates nor Balbuk was alive to see it, but Balbuk's refusal to be ignored and the records

Bates kept of Balbuk's clan territory helped the Federal Court to rule in 2006 that native title continued to exist in Perth, the first time such a claim had been upheld in an Australian capital city. Balbuk died in 1907. There is a photograph of her as an older woman against a backdrop of scrub. She is wearing a chaste ankle-length skirt and a long-sleeved white shirt buttoned to her neck, her face framed by long grey hair, but the image captures the pride and defiance in her eyes.

Where I stand in the south-eastern corner of the fifteenth floor, I can clearly follow Balbuk's route from the edge of the CBD at the Causeway, past the Governor's residence, heading north up Barrack Street towards the Perth train station that was built on the reclaimed freshwater lake. Balbuk's story has always been a reminder to me that beneath the geometric frame of the modern city – the bar-graph rectangles of concrete, glass and steel across the skyline – there exist footpads worn smooth over millennia that snake up through the sheoak and marri woodland and into the city's heart. I have found myself in other cities, on other continents, seated on park benches or riding the trains, thinking about Fanny Balbuk, keeping to her straight track through the streets of Perth.

Fanny Balbuk's yearning for what had been taken from her is very different from the yearning of mid-twentieth-century Perth for what it might become: the City of Light whose significance, its burghers hoped, could no longer be ignored. The first sign of the tension between the city's aspirations and the relaxed lives of its inhabitants surfaced after Perth's gesture of solidarity with an American astronaut in February 1962. John Glenn was solo-orbiting Earth, a fellow traveller on the dark edge of what was known. Perth kept its lights on overnight to keep the lonely Glenn company, but this action triggered a latent desire to be noticed, and admired, that became a source of amusement to many of Perth's citizens.

Perth in 1962 was a small city blessed with natural riches but not much wealth. Its isolation from the eastern states was keenly felt: Perth had only been connected by trunk line since 1930 and by train since 1917; flights were expensive. It was beside the point that the 'City of Light' title bestowed upon Perth put the city in competition with Paris, which had earned the name as a centre for new ideas during the Enlightenment. What mattered was that John Glenn had seen Perth from outer space, and he was grateful. I was told this story as a child with the stress absolutely on Glenn's courage, drifting alone in a capsule through the darkness of space. It was clear from the telling that Perth's desire to comfort Glenn was born purely out of a spirit of camaraderie (not for our military ally, but for the astronaut), although this was only the beginning of the story.

The tale of isolated Perth and what was perceived to be its generous act went viral, by the standards of the early 1960s. Jenny Gregory is a Winthrop Professor of History at the University of Western Australia, and in *City of Light: A History of Perth Since the 1950s* she notes that unknown Perth was exposed to prime-time network television audiences in the United States and was mentioned in *The New York Times*. Western Australia's premier, David Brand, had been enthusiastic about allowing the streetlights to burn all night, but Perth's mayor, Harry Howard, had not. In fact, he was quoted in the afternoon paper the *Daily News* as stating that because of the costs involved the idea was 'morally wrong'. Prior to the astronaut's flyover, the front-page headline thundered, 'It's a Waste, Says Howard.'

But then the letters of thanks started pouring in from the United States, which put Mayor

Howard in an awkward position. Jenny Gregory points out the resulting 'great attitudinal' gulf, listing some of the patriotic and grateful correspondence from abroad in contrast to the satirical ditties sung around Perth and Paul Rigby's biting cartoons in the *Daily News*. According to Gregory, Howard was receiving letters asking for his 'photo, his autograph, even a button from his shirt'.

Author Ron Davidson, now in his early eighties and one of the city's great raconteurs, recently reminded me that 'Perth was always a city full of cheeky people', and so it was. Things just got better for the eager satirists when Mayor Howard accepted an invitation from the mayor of New York to attend John Glenn's ticker-tape parade through Manhattan.

Howard, in his full mayoral regalia, was feted by the crowd of four million who turned out to cheer Glenn. He was placed in the third car of the procession, behind only the astronaut and US president John F. Kennedy. Robert Drewe's 1986 novel *Fortune* describes the mayor on his own relative journey into intercontinental space: 'no astronaut was more overwhelmed by the emotion of the occasion, or waved and smiled more heartily at the cheering New Yorkers ... As his city beamed up at gallant John Glenn, so he beamed up at the towers of Wall Street.'

After such heady days, it must have been hard for Howard to return to his asbestos and tin city visible to the world only from outer space. Howard tried to lure Glenn to Perth by sending him a photo of Tania Verstak, Miss Australia 1961 and Miss International 1962, 'so that you can see your image has been admired by someone of exceptional beauty, and she is indeed typical of our Australian girls'. Journalist Michael Charlton might have declaimed, 'Fair Tania, you make the bright sun seem dim,' but the rather sad strategy failed – although for a while money dribbled in from Yanks eager to 'help pay the light bill'.

As I look across at the glass towers of Perth's business heart, St Georges Terrace, I'm reminded of the news trumpeted in the morning paper that fifty years after Mayor Howard's journey to Manhattan, the mountain is finally coming to Mohammed: Wall Street investment banking firm Goldman Sachs is opening a Perth office. The article was accompanied by breathless descriptions of Perth's new charms, the regeneration of the CBD with swanky restaurants and niche bars and cosmopolitan festival events, and the new confidence that the city might be shaking off its 'Dullsville' tag. But there is ambivalence, too, at the growing pains that are also evident: rumours that the numbers of people arriving weekly are being downplayed; the scale of the suburban sprawl; the newly clogged roads and expense of basic foodstuffs; the fear that affluence is exhibited in ways that diminish rather than enhance community – bigger cars, bigger boats, bigger houses, higher walls.

The lights of the city have come on in dazzling fluorescent straps, spreading out from the CBD along sulphur-lit arteries. They make it easier to see the four spokes of the growth corridors that spread in long suburban chains north-west towards Joondalup, north-east towards Ellenbrook, south-east towards Armadale and south-west towards Mandurah. Until recently Perth was the fastest-growing capital city in Australia, courtesy of the latest mining boom, and most of the growth is suburban.

The first mining boom, in the 1890s, cycled 500 000 people through a city that until then consisted of 48 000 colonists. Tens of thousands of men and women camped in tent cities located at Claisebrook near the Causeway and in parts of Fremantle. Victorian (or t'othersider) communities soon emerged in what are today the inner-city suburbs of Subiaco, Victoria Park and North Perth, while more established residents tended to stay near the river.

Now there are suburbs on the margins of the city that I've never heard of, and my three-year-old street directory is hopelessly out of date. In one or two of the newer suburbs I've driven through, the fast-food infrastructure has been completed but the franchises remain surrounded by acres of sand, waiting for the people to come. In other subdivisions, ye olde Potemkin village centres have been plonked down among the suburban streets, seemingly overnight, a sleight of hand designed to evoke memories of community from other places.

From the heights, Perth is a densely treed landscape. The only exception is the white stucco blocks of Northbridge at my feet, port of call for so many migrant communities over the years. The notorious old slums of East Perth up the road (where the population density in the early twentieth century was double that of Sydney's Paddington) have been redeveloped. The edges of the CBD are defined to the east by the 1960s curves of the Police Headquarters and to the west by Parliament House, severed from the city by the high walls of the sunken Mitchell Freeway. Some of the earliest

Georgian buildings erected by the first settlers are still there, albeit dwarfed by glass towers, as are some of the convict-built civic structures and gold-rush Victorian buildings of the 1890s.

It occurs to me now, up here, that if the first iron-ore boom had happened in the 1920s rather than the 1960s, Perth might have closely resembled golden-age Los Angeles, whose Mediterranean climate it shares. We might have graceful Art Deco towers rather than the beige office blocks that largely replaced the 'Parisian' streetscape of the 1900s St Georges Terrace. Art Deco suits Perth's pure light, and like the Art Deco movement, with its optimism for a shiny humanist future brighter than what eventuated, Perth has also been a city cast in the shadow of its promise and potential – the enduring fever-dream of the City of Light.

As a result, Perth is a city of great contradictions. Statistics tell us that it's the sunniest of all Australian capitals, and that it has proportionally the highest number of boat owners and backyard swimming pools. But Perth also has the highest rates of incarceration, with nearly half of those imprisoned being Aboriginal people, and one of the highest rates of homelessness. Perth is the capital city with the highest proportion of residents born overseas (forty-one per cent), although roughly one-third of these migrants came from Britain, Ireland, New Zealand and South Africa (a similarly large number are from South-east Asia). It is a city with low unemployment and high wages for skilled workers, yet much of this depends upon the volatile mining sector. The two-speed economy generated by the latest boom affects the cost of living for all residents, making life tough for those who aren't well paid.

Perth is often described as the world's most isolated capital city. It's a title less relevant than it was for most of the twentieth century, when flying interstate was expensive and the Nullarbor Plain was crossed via dirt track. Before the 1890s gold rush, people didn't see themselves as being isolated from the eastern states, where almost nobody came from (because nobody wanted to come). Instead they measured distance from the mother country, and of course Perth is closer to Britain than either Sydney or Melbourne. Perth became by definition an isolated provincial capital after Federation in 1901, only eleven years after the colony had been granted self-government, and only thirty-odd years before it tried to secede from Australia. During the Depression years of the 1930s, it was felt that the 'Hume Highway Hegemony' of Canberra–Sydney–Melbourne wasn't acting in Western Australia's best interests.

As historian Geoffrey Bolton points out in *Land of Vision and Mirage*, the effect of the first sixty years of Perth's isolated existence, before the first wave of migration from the eastern states in the 1890s, needn't be overstated. Yet it's there in the language, in the roughly 750 distinctively used words, such as 'verge' for nature strip, 'crosswalk' for zebra crossing and 'brook' for small stream, and Nyungar words such as 'boondy' for small stone (sand-boondies are what kids throw at each other in the playground or on building sites) and 'gidgee' for Hawaiian sling/spear, none of which made it across the Nullarbor.

The effect of isolation is also there in the contrarian spirit that saw Perth rail against the perceived disinterest of the British government for most of the nineteenth century, and against Canberra since 1901, resulting in the belief that, according to Bolton:

> in their isolated community, disagreements should never be pushed too far, but all should stick together. No doubt this was convenient to those

who wielded political and economic power ...
and no doubt troublemakers and dissenters often
found it hard to gain a serious hearing, but this
clannish sense of fundamentally shared identity of
interest seems to have formed an effective social
cement.

If anything, Perth's distance from the other Australian cities fostered a spirit of making-do and innovation. The city may remain on the margins of the national consciousness, but I suspect that this is of little concern to most residents, if only because modern Perth is a city that doesn't look in on itself. The sky that fills so much of any view across the city, the ocean horizon, the lowness and roundedness of the ancient hills – all induce an outward-looking frame of mind and a corresponding awareness of other lives and places.

There's also something about Perth's isolation that paradoxically diminishes any sense of real physical distance. Sometimes you forget that the nearest cities are many hours' drive away to the south and north, and that the nearest capital city is more than 2000 kilometres away – not a great deal fewer than Perth's favourite overseas holiday destination in Indonesia. This, coupled with the time it takes to get anywhere else, has accustomed us to a love of the journey, an easy*goingness* inspired by a nonchalance about distance. Even distant cities on distant continents never seem too far away, merely just over the horizon, like everything else.

A city with porous boundaries, Perth has rarely contained the desires of its younger citizens, many of whom journey to find experience elsewhere, while a large population of workers commute hundreds, sometimes thousands of kilometres to their workplaces. This is only the latest expression of a mobile urban population that has always had strong social links to those who live 'in the country' or 'on the mines'. It's a mobility that reinforces the sense that largely suburban Perth sits easily upon the land, and on occasions feels as ephemeral as an encampment.

From the fifteenth storey, too, I'm reminded that Perth is a city of arcades: shaded strips over narrow paths running right through the city from south to north. I fondly remember my visits as a child from the mining towns of the north-west: the thrilling pressure of human traffic funnelled through the arcades in what was otherwise a lifetime lived outdoors, the close smells of cooking and perfume and multicultural humanity captured within the cool and noisy tunnels that echoed to your shout.

The arcades are a hangover from the initial surveying of the city in that first year of settlement, 1829, by John Septimus Roe. Perth was the first colonial city in Australia built to a plan, and the plan dictated an orthogonal shape parallel to the Swan River foreshore, defined by town blocks subdivided into ten allotments. There were strict rules as to the placing of buildings set back from the verge. The prohibitions against the unnecessary cutting down of native trees meant that in many respects Perth began its life resembling the contemporary garden suburbs that surround its city hub now.

Although the early European colonists were often disappointed with the conditions awaiting them at the mouth of the Swan River, in the port settlement of Fremantle, time and again their narratives became rhapsodic upon entering the river in one of the lighters, or barges able to negotiate the banks and spits of the frequent shallows, especially at the narrow channel between Chidley Point and Blackwall Reach. There, the first signs that they were entering a different world altogether: the high walls of craggy limestone rising above them, then the steeply wooded hillsides and rush-lined foreshores of Freshwater Bay and Melville Water; the sight of black swans, pelicans and cormorants drying their wings; avocets, stilts and dotterels wading in the shallows; the colourful spray of wildflowers beneath the sheoak, marri and jarrah woodland canopy. On the left flank rose the heights of Mount Eliza, crested with woodland forest, the river lapping at its base, concealing and then revealing the small settlement of Perth as they poled into Mounts Bay.

Before them stood a village of large plots and sandy streets, reed huts and canvas tents. Vines had already been planted on the flats by the waterline. Ahead of them lay Heirisson Island, and behind its mudflats flowed Clause Brook, with its adjacent freshwater lagoon and fringe of giant banksia and thirty-foot zamia palms. To the north, the settlement was corralled by a hidden chain of wetland lakes, while beyond was the floodplain around Maylands and the serpentine river narrowing as it descended from the third port of Guildford; the low blue rise of the scarp running in a cambered ridgeline across the eastern horizon.

Perth village in 1829 was a place, according to one observer, where few went to bed sober. It's hard to know what 'Old Yellagonga', the Whadjuk custodian of the Perth area, which the Nyungar called Boorloo, must have made of the comings and goings of the people before him as he watched from his camp at Byerbup on the hill near Mount Eliza. A majority of the settlers were in their twenties and thirties. Many of the women were pregnant, and most had children. Down on the waterline they carried their canvas-wrapped goods across the mudflats of Mounts Bay, breaking the mirror surface with their poles and paddles, past the private boat of Governor James Stirling's wife, Ellen, with its blue and red bunting that so excited the children.

From his position on the hill, Yellagonga had a clear line of sight to where Roe stalked the sand to mark out the allotments, across from the red clay bricks laid in grids to dry in the sun, the nets of the fishermen drawing in tonnes of bony herring and mullet, the drunks singing in the window-less tavern at night, the pigs and sheep and cows lowing in their pens, and the planting of crops on land that Yellagonga knew would soon be flooded.

Yellagonga, who had hunting rights to the northern wetlands through his wife, Yingani, was soon to be displaced from his favourite camp by the soldiers of the 63rd Regiment. He was forced to move his people out to Lake Monger, where they received rations of rice and flour. The practice was designed to discourage them from the new settlement, because of their mostly naked appearance and 'quarrelsome nature'.

Yellagonga appears to have been well liked by the citizens of the colony, and an 1843 obituary in one of the village's first newspapers, *The Perth Gazette*, described him as 'mild and amiable'. However, Robert Menli Lyon, a young Scot who was drawn to empathise with the plight of the Whadjuk people, and warriors Yagan and Midgegooroo in particular, considered that Yellagonga was a fitting tribal elder, because 'when fully roused, no warrior, not even Yagan, dare stand before him'. Despite this, Lyon was also to write that due to Yellagonga's benevolent nature, 'the settlers are greatly indebted for the protection of their lives and property'.

Neither Yellagonga nor the settlers who displaced his clan were to know that within the first year, which saw thirty-six ships arrive, bringing 2000 new arrivals to the colony, many of whom were to depart in disgust to the colonies further east, the arrivals would suddenly cease and there would be no net population increase for the next decade. Convicts arrived in large numbers in 1849, and their labour transformed Perth from a Georgian village into a small Victorian town: its buildings marooned amid streets of sand, so that in early photographs the town appears like a museum set-piece, or a diorama, or even a ghost town. Otherwise, Perth would grow slowly until the 1890s, with the coming of the first mining boom.

Those citizens who endured the first fifty years, who might also be described as shareholders, were participants in the creation of a city that, 190 years later, pushing energetically and destructively out at its margins into the banksia woodland, still maintains that initial aura described by artist and illustrator Shaun Tan, when he speaks of Perth's 'shoreline of light, space and restless silence'.

The River

'Thank God we don't outlive all of our childhood fancies.'

Tim Winton, *Land's Edge*

Once a day, the skin of the Swan River rises in a small ripple as the tidal surge makes its way from the river mouth at Fremantle through Perth Water and up into the higher reaches of the river near the fast-growing suburb of Ellenbrook, just over twenty kilometres north-east of Perth. In winter, when a layer of brackish water runs off the scarp towards the ocean, the river flows in two directions, with the fresh water flowing seawards above the saline water flowing in beneath it.

Today the diurnal bulge of water that reveals the incoming tide is invisible. It's a Sunday morning and I'm out on the river in an open kayak with my Uncle Scott, my father's youngest brother.

Scott moved from Tasmania to Perth as a teenager in the 1970s. Like so many others, he stayed for the climate and the lifestyle and the opportunity to work.

We put in to the river at Middle Swan and slowly glide our way upstream towards Ellen Brook, which takes its name from Captain James Stirling's young bride. This part of the river marks the furthest point that Stirling reached during his reconnoitre of 1827, with his small crew in one of the HMS *Success*'s longboats, not knowing if he would get the opportunity to return.

Stirling had married Ellen Mangles, the daughter of a wealthy merchant with links to the East India Company, in 1823. He was thirty-two and she was sixteen. The story goes that Stirling first came across Ellen as a young teen, her feet astride two bareback horses, reins in her left and right hands, the nineteenth-century equivalent of hooning on her father's estate.

Portraits of Stirling as a young man emphasise his dark eyes; his grim, almost bitter mouth; and the stiff military posture expected of an officer. He'd joined the navy at the age of twelve, but he was an ambitious thirty-six-year-old when he was posted to Sydney in 1826. He convinced New

South Wales governor Ralph Darling to allow him to survey the Swan River, although he was not the first European to visit the area.

In 1616 Dutchman Dirk Hartog surveyed the western coast of Australia and by 1627 Rottnest Island appeared on the first maps. The first reports of the Swan River were made in 1697 by fellow Dutchman Willem de Vlamingh's party, who entered the river and journeyed as far as the Causeway flats. While de Vlamingh is mostly remembered for naming Perth's favourite holiday island *Rats-nest* (after the marsupial quokka), an island that he found to be a 'terrestrial paradise ... delightful above all others I've seen', he also named the river *Swartte Swanne Drift* (Black Swan River). Representative of the fabulousness of European imaginings of the Great Southern Land at the time, de Vlamingh wrote that based on his discovery of 'gigantic human footprints ... That river leads to a land inhabited by giants.'

More than a century later, the French arrived in Western Australian waters as part of an expedition to map the coastline of the continent. In 1801 Sub-lieutenant Francois-Antoine Boniface Heirisson of the *Naturaliste* was commanded to take a longboat and explore the estuary and upper reaches of the Swan River. Post-Enlightenment explorers the Frenchmen might have been, part of the largest scientific team to ever leave Europe, but they were also chary of visiting a land where, according to academic Ross Gibson, there existed birds that didn't fly, rivers that flowed inland, and wood that didn't float. It must have seemed a bad omen when huge sharks circled their longboat en route from the *Naturaliste* to the river mouth (they caught one, a fourteen-footer). They were prepared for the worst, arming themselves with a small cannon and a musket for each man.

Inside the estuary, Heirisson was impressed. The area was densely wooded, with 'beautiful flowering shrubs', and the black swans were edible. Near the muddy, mosquito-ridden surrounds of the island that now bears Heirisson's name, the men did indeed identify a giant's footprint, which led to them doubling their sentries and burning bonfires through the night. However, it wasn't until they were further upriver that they were greeted 'by the most heart-chilling howls, so close that they seemed to emanate from the reeds,' Heirisson wrote. 'Feeling at a disadvantage under the cover of darkness, against an adversary whether man or beast, we chose to remain in mid-stream – where we spent a wretched night under the teeming rain.'

Twenty-seven years later, following his own inspection of the area, Stirling knew that London was the best place to influence those who might realise his project: a colony on the Swan River that he suggested calling Hesperia, 'indicating a Country looking towards the Setting Sun'. He was in luck. The Duke of Wellington became prime minister of Britain in 1828, and one of Stirling's old Scottish familial allies, the member for Perth in the national parliament, Sir George Murray, was named Minister for War and the Colonies. With a scratch of Murray's quill, the settlement scheme was on. Stirling would later repay those who had made the venture possible by naming the settlement Perth (the alternative proposed was Kingston) and its main thoroughfares Wellington, Murray and Hay streets (the third after Colonial Under-Secretary Robert Hay, the public servant who'd supported Stirling).

As is the case with any real estate venture today, flyers were immediately circulated and advertisements were taken out. The resulting 'Swan River Mania', as it was described in British newspapers, came down to Stirling tapping into the desires of a motivated caste of largely urban Britons:

adventurers and those who would these days be called the 'aspirational class' – those wealthy enough to emigrate but not so rich that they might be insulated from the difficult economic conditions of the period.

We paddle quietly past the newly restored All Saints Church in Henley Brook, made of local mud bricks and oyster-shell lime. It is the oldest – and perhaps the smallest – church in Perth. Adorned with a simple bellcote, the church was built to mark the place where Stirling had prayed with his men in 1827 before returning downriver. In his journal, Stirling described how

> the richness of the soil, the bright foliage of
> the shrubs, the majesty of the surrounding
> trees, the abrupt and red colour banks of the
> river occasionally seen, and the view of the blue
> mountains, from which we were not far distant,
> made the scenery of this spot as bieutiful [*sic*] as
> anything of the kind I have ever witnessed.

For us, too, it's a beautiful spring morning and the river is peaceful and the muddy banks high.

You can smell the bricks baking at the local works and hear the drone of traffic on Reid Highway, but there is nobody else on the water. We pass some of Australia's oldest vineyards – Houghton and Sandalford – and dozens of newer ones, part of the original allotments disbursed by Surveyor-General Roe. The dry winter has limited the run-off from the Swan/Avon catchment (the Avon, Canning and Helena rivers are the Swan's three main tributaries), and while the water is brackish rather than saline, there is little flow to breach the incoming tide.

The tidal influence is felt right up to Ellen Brook, so the birdlife is similar to the lower estuary; there are shags and pelicans in large numbers, which suggests that there are plentiful fish but also that the river is more saline than usual. In a winter of heavy rain, practically the whole of the Swan River estuary is flushed out with fresh water and the more freshwater-intolerant fish are forced to migrate out into the ocean for a time. A neighbour of mine who works for the Swan River Trust told me that the Swan River bull sharks pup in the upper river during spring, and that one of their main food sources is birdlife. The pelicans and cormorants look unconcerned.

The shags move about like sticks thrown from tree to tree, or settle on pontoons and jetties to dry their wings. I've always been fascinated by the shag, the generic term for the four types of cormorant and one species of darter found on the Swan. When I was a child spear-fishing in the river, nervous of dark shadowy shapes, it was common to see a shag glide into a school of mullet or trumpeter beneath me, often many at the same time. Sometimes shags hunt communally, and because their feathers contain no protective oils (although strangely for this reason they look like the greasiest of birds) they spend a fair proportion of their time perched on rocks or branches with their sodden black wings comically draped in the sunshine, like skinny angels.

Novelist Seaforth Mackenzie wrote beautifully about this section of the upper river from his perspective as a boarder at Guildford Grammar, the same private boys' school where my younger brother learnt everything he needed to survive some tough years in the army. The first time I read Mackenzie's 1937 novel *The Young Desire It*, I identified with his narrator, a shy boy prone to spending time alone by the river. His budding sexuality is reflected in his observations of the waters, where the 'air was warm and sweet with the rotting water-levels of winter floods. Snags thrust up above their brown reflections ... drying and crusted with their own watery decay, but hard as iron beneath, and slippery to the swimmer's naked foot.'

I didn't go to a private boarding school, but the dislocation that Mackenzie's narrator feels when removed from his mother's rural property was something I understood. Our family had moved from the Pilbara, in the north of Western Australia, to Perth in 1976. Because of my father's employment in the Royal Australian Air Force, and later in the mining game, my mother estimates that in my first ten years we moved some twenty-one times before we finally settled in Perth.

We were used to moving interstate and overseas, from air force base to small country town, but this was the first time I remember feeling any degree of culture shock. In the city, kids wore socks and shoes rather than getting about barefoot. They spoke a strange coded language gleaned from a popular culture that was alien to me. The air was heavy and damp (my sister recalls the 'uncomfortable feeling' that she was unable to articulate at the time, as it was so alien to us, of 'being cold'), and the suburbs stretched endlessly on our weekend drives up into the hills.

So the river was a haven for me. It was a place that reminded me of the one I'd left behind, where spiders and goannas and parrots and eagles had ruled the gullies, mud crabs and hermit crabs and mudskippers had populated the mangroves, and wild donkeys and kangaroos had filled the spaces now taken up by people. It was in the yellow sands and quarried limestone crags and bronzed shallows that I felt most at home as a child newly arrived from the desert. Here my brother and I dug out cave cubbies from the banks of sand. We hunted rabbits with bows and arrows, we speared cobbler, and we paddled out on surfboards into the broader river.

I can still remember the moment when I was suddenly happy to be in Perth, when I first felt like I belonged to my new home. It was an early summer morning on an incoming tide and I was alone in the water. I must have been about twelve or thirteen. Walking along the muddy foreshore, I'd seen the imprints of flathead in perfect moulds at low tide, the fan shape of their side-fins and the great weight of their spotted flanks, the broad-arrow indentation of their cavernous mouths at rest. I'd become fascinated by this lurking predator, as I would later become fascinated by the kingie, or mulloway, and later still sharks, finding as many books and speaking to as many fishermen and women as I could on the subject.

I'd caught a few flathead on a line from jetties but they were nowhere near the size I'd witnessed in lies left in the squelchy mud. Armed with a gidgee, I swam out into the current and drifted over the local sandbank at high tide, with its wave-rippled skin and sea-lettuce tumbleweed, anticipating the flathead lying in wait for the school-fish who fed in the shallows. And they were, camouflaged against the speckled mud, watchful as my shadow drifted across them. I was able to remain immobile except for my shivering, and let the current carry me – relaxed and concentrating at the same time. The large brown *Phyllorhiza punctata* and the smaller white *Aurelia aurita* jellyfish drifted with me and around me, my fellow travellers in the tidal current.

In her novel *Black Mirror*, Gail Jones describes the jellyfish as 'fruit bowls pulsating above her, light caught semi-circular in their fleshy domes … she half expected to see a baby-face heave jellyfish-like into view', while Robert Drewe in his novel *The*

Drowner describes them undulating 'below the surface as if swaying under glass. In their translucent but individually patterned globes the urgent faces of unborn babies press up against the ceiling.' These images of gestation would have appealed to me as a child, fascinated by the strange mobility of an unboned creature in an amniotic brine. The jellyfish were sometimes so numerous in the shallows that you could swim through them and upon them – the tactile nudge and little shiver of pleasure and revulsion as they brushed against my belly, face and legs.

This was a time in my life when, to use author Brenda Walker's expression, I lived within 'a loose muscular happiness that [my] mind was going to have trouble catching up with', except that it did, and too soon, leaving me with only the memory of the small epiphany I had that morning floating in the river: the sunlight burning my naked back, illuminating the algae-rich shallows; the gobble-guts, blowies and hardyheads accustomed to my presence. As a giant flathead spurted away into the darkness leaving a trail of smuts like a departing steam train, all of the sensual confusion of cold water and hot sun, and levitation and submersion, came together in a sudden recognition that I have never forgotten: the feeling of belonging to a place that did not belong to me, but only made an introverted kid feel more protective, even loving, of the river that carried him along on its soft skin.

About a kilometre downstream from Ellen Brook, the still surface of the river becomes covered in the delicate white flowers of the flooded gum, while beside us cicadas work up a racket and a whistling kite swoops over to take a look. It isn't hard to imagine the river as a billabong, so still and quiet in the midday heat, or as a place where restless spirits reside. I was a boy brought up on the stories of May Gibbs, who lived in Perth as a young girl and teenager. Her gumnut babies were inspired by the fruits of the marri tree, and her Wicked Banksia Men were created when, as a child out walking in the Western Australian bush, she came across 'a grove of banksia trees, and sitting on almost every branch were these ugly little, wicked men'.

For a boy newly arrived to Perth, swimming in this part of the river always unnerved me, especially treading water in the pools dark with leaf litter and laterite alluvium, the shaded banks and strange cold currents tugging at my feet, the unusual lack of buoyancy. My parents had all the illustrated Ainslie Roberts and Charles Mountford books on Aboriginal mythology, and I remember watching the Swan River frothing over rock pools within a forest of sloughing wind and granite boulders, sacred kingfishers swooping dragonflies over the tannic water, and being reminded of Roberts' pictures of dreaming landscapes, with their dramatic images of mythological characters. There was something about the resin-smelling water and lemony sunlight and humid dampness of the forest floor that evoked a sense of the uncanny. This impression was accentuated on our way home through the town of Guildford and its surrounding suburbs, although the mythos belonged to a different culture and a different time.

Just as it was affecting to see the Swan River in the hills so different from its long flat lower reaches, it was always odd to pass through Guildford on the same journey and be reminded of the illustrations of Tarry Town in Washington Irving's short story 'The Legend of Sleepy Hollow'. Guildford was so unlike the open country and spreading suburbs I knew further west: everything seemed smaller and older, more like a medieval market village. The air was cooler and even the sky lower. Shadows were darker. There was dampness. The homes seemed snug and their yards resembled the cottage gardens of an English county village. The narrow river passed beneath a small jarrah bridge. It wasn't hard to imagine a headless horseman and to relocate the stories of English highwaymen that I so enjoyed.

My impressions of Guildford and nearby Bassendean were always fleeting, made on trips to the footy and passing through to the hills. I usually only met kids from the hills at youth camps or football carnivals, and I was always aware that they seemed tougher than lowlanders. They spoke of owning rifles and motorbikes, like country kids. Their playground wasn't the ocean but the expanse of bush on the other side of the scarp. I was always jealous of their freedom, which reminded me of my time in the Pilbara.

In a Judah Waten short story, 'To a Country Town', first published in 1947, the narrator's father is a disappointed migrant in 'a very hard, inhospitable land for a Jew to live in'. In contrast to the myth he'd been sold before his arrival of 'a country bathed in gold', he reflects that in the hills of Perth, he'd discovered 'such poverty ... that it would make your hair stand on end'. This is the older persona of the Perth hills, an area more usually represented as a place of quiet beauty and solitude, a refuge for lowlanders looking to get away from the city, a spot for picnics (which it always was for us as kids) and weekenders. But Judah Waten's family soon found a community in the hills, where the poverty and hardship created a working-class camaraderie that defined the local culture more than ethnicity or religion. It's the kind of culture that shaped the man that celebrated economist Nugget Coombs would become, for example, and it's expressed in the short stories of Katharine Susannah Prichard and the tough-minded paintings by former German prisoner-of-war camp inmate Guy Grey-Smith.

The hills have also existed as a respite for those who don't quite fit into the lowland suburban culture of greater Perth, people who might want to do things differently: bikies, artists, hippies and tree-changers, among others. As a result, the tough kids from the hills I met on camps were always hard to reconcile with my naive picture of wildflower season in the national parks that ridge the scarp, just as it was always hard to reconcile my picture of the slow, shallow Swan River near Guildford with what I knew was a river prone to severe flooding.

We were taught in school that during the 1926 flood the Swan River broke its banks and spread five kilometres across the fertile floodplain of the Swan Valley, while downriver the same flood took out the original Fremantle Railway Bridge only moments after a train had passed over it. The first recorded flood was in 1830, when the river rose 6.1 metres above its normal level. The floods continued regularly right up to the 1960s, by which time the river had been properly 'trained' to course along dredged channels that originate on the scarp near Northam and Toodyay, north-east of Perth, down to its mouth at Fremantle.

In the early 1960s, when my father was a new arrival at the Pearce Air Force Base, he was washed away in one of these intermittent floods. The base is north of Perth and my father had been eager to get into the city for an appointment. Upon seeing the stalled traffic and the swollen river washing over the bridge, he asked a local truck driver whether his Volkswagen Beetle might make it across. The truck driver, obviously noticing that my crew-cut father with Victorian plates was a t'othersider, gamely suggested that he might 'give it a go'. But as soon as the Beetle entered the waters, its wheels lifted and it was carried downriver. Water gushed into the car past the brake and clutch pedals, the car tipped forwards, and my father thought he was about to die.

Fortunately, the river deposited the car on a knoll in a paddock downstream before it could tumble underwater. When my father turned on the windscreen wipers, he saw that a horse was staring at him from only feet away. My father wound down the windows and opened the car doors and waited until all of the water had drained out, turned the ignition key, and miraculously started the car. He then drove out of the paddock, with the horse following him.

This flood was almost as bad as the 1926 flood. According to the records, the 1963 flood caused families in the Guildford area to be evacuated, and the river ran high and brackish for two months. The 280-kilometre-long Avon/Swan River has a catchment area of some 193 000 square kilometres, much of which derives from the salt-lake country on the scarp, and the Avon River in particular is quite saline, where the Canning is fresh.

If Guildford and the Swan Valley seemed ripe for me to populate with mythological figures, this was because of my passion for all things bushranger. One of the first books my mother gave me was an illustrated history of Australian bushrangers, and I loved the reckless life of the men and women on the run. This fascination only grew once I came across the figure of Joseph Bolitho Johns, or Moondyne Joe as he's commonly known in Perth. He's named after the river-valley region beyond the Perth hills where he spent much of his time.

Moondyne Joe probably wouldn't have made the illustrated Australian bushrangers book, even in the unlikely event that the publishers had been interested in areas outside Victoria and New South Wales. Moondyne Joe never killed anyone. He never held up a stagecoach or waged a pitched gun battle with coppers. Nor was he ever really 'a terror to the rich man', although like many of my childhood heroes he did have a passion for fast horses.

Moondyne Joe was the subject of the first novel written about Western Australia, *Moondyne: A Story of Convict Life in Western Australia*, published in 1879 (although banned in Perth during his lifetime). However, it's fair to say that the historical

Moondyne Joe and the fictional Moondyne are wildly different. The novel was written by John Boyle O'Reilly, a man equally admired in Western Australian folklore as the subject of his novel. He's remembered in Perth as a Fenian prisoner who escaped the Western Australian convict system to organise a rescue mission for his comrades. Their escape was celebrated in the banned song 'The Catalpa' that was still being sung a hundred years later; we learnt it at my local primary school, as did every Perth kid of my generation.

O'Reilly's novel is the kind of colonial 'lost world' adventure later popularised by H. Rider Haggard. Moondyne is taken in by local Aboriginal people, who make him their king and reveal to him a cave stuffed with gold. But wealth is not Moondyne's real focus and he returns to Britain, where he becomes a successful penal reformer.

The historical Moondyne Joe's adventures and achievements were far more modest, although it's precisely their human scale that made him such a significant cultural figure to the inhabitants of Perth. Moondyne Joe's crimes included stealing a horse, petty thieving while on the lam, and allegedly killing an ox. There were escaped convicts who shot police and died violently, but their names have been forgotten; another convict bushranger, Frank Hall, spent time with Nyungar people in the south-west but little is known about him now. Moondyne Joe's real legacy was his contribution to the satirical urges of his Swan River compatriots and their feelings of resentment towards Governor John Hampton in particular.

Hampton arrived in Perth in 1862 with an already tarnished reputation. He was alleged to have profited from the misuse of convict labour in his previous posting in Tasmania, and he had initially defended the brutal commandant at Norfolk Island, John Price. In Robert Hughes's account of the early history of Australia, *The Fatal Shore*, Hughes describes Hampton as 'a dismally cynical opportunist' whose practices were 'odious and corrupt'.

According to historian Ian Elliot, the number of convict escapes rose significantly during Hampton's harsh tenure in Perth. In one nine-month period between 1866 and 1867, ninety made their getaway, although all were soon recaptured and no doubt flogged. There were some 12 800 lashes of the cat-o'-nine-tails delivered during the convict years; every one of them, according to Fenian prisoner Thomas McCarthy Fennell, tore the flesh until 'ghastly flow the purple fluids from the mangled pulp'. During the construction of the Fremantle Bridge, so many men bolted that a large area of scrub was cleared nearby and extra guards were needed. The regular firing of a warning cannon at Fremantle Prison proved highly unpopular, because, according to *The Perth Gazette*, it played 'sad havoc' with the town windows.

Moondyne Joe, comfortable in the bush of the Avon Valley and the Perth hills, was able to elude capture longer than any other escaped convict. He was rumoured to be living with the Ballardong Nyungar and ranging between many of the landmarks that now bear his name. He once survived for two years on the run within Perth's small community, who never gave him up despite the large reward. In doing so, Moondyne Joe showed how one might disrupt the disparity of power between a famously cruel, unpopular governor and a powerless and often chained illiterate labourer from Cornwall, who had been sentenced to transportation for possessing stolen cheese, bread and mutton. He embarked on a series of minor actions that drew popular support away from the rulers and towards the lowest caste in white society during that period: the convict.

Moondyne Joe's exploits came at a time when, according to the polemic of one Fenian prisoner quoted in historian Simon Adams' *The Unforgiving Rope*, 'more real depravity, more shocking wickedness, more undisguised vice and immorality is to be witnessed at midday in the most public thoroughfares of Perth, with its population of 1500, than in any other city of fifty times its population, either in Europe or America'. If this is to be believed, the nostalgic dreams of the early settlers to re-create a vanishing English way of life had never been more distant, although the citizens of Perth circa 1862 were greatly entertained by their favourite bushranger.

You can hear the glee in the most famous of the satirical ditties sung around Perth at the time: 'The governor's son has got the pip, the governor's got the measles, but Moondyne Joe has given 'em the slip, pop goes the weasel'. However, there was nothing funny about the special cell built for Moondyne Joe at Fremantle Prison on the orders of Governor Hampton. It was a lightless slot reinforced with jarrah sleepers and iron spikes, and to this day it's a popular exhibit on the somewhat ghoulish Fremantle Prison tour that also takes in the death row cells, the whipping frame and the hangman's scaffold. Neither was there anything funny about the months Joe spent in this cell, nor the fact that, as reported in *The Perth Gazette* of 12 October 1862, Hampton had personally visited the prison for the express purpose of seeing Joe in chains. The governor had subsequently returned to his residence, the new Government House, 'with his mind in its normal state of placidity'.

There *is* something comical, however, about Hampton's hubristic goad that should Joe ever escape the custom-built cell, he would receive a pardon. This throwaway challenge is the pivot on which the legend of Moondyne Joe turns, because this is precisely what happened next. At risk of dying in his slot, Joe was allowed out of the cell, but only to break rocks in the sun. He did this very skilfully and with a surprising enthusiasm: the pile of limestone rubble built daily until finally it obscured Joe from the nearby guard. Joe had been slyly taking a pick to the prison wall. After constructing an effective dummy out of scavenged wire, a pick and his prison smock, he escaped semi-naked and eluded the authorities until he was finally caught trying to steal wine from Houghton vineyard. He was thrown back into Fremantle Prison, although the new governor,

Frederick Weld, upon hearing of his predecessor's promise, released Joe on parole.

Sadly, little is known about Joe's later life, except that his brief good fortune soured after he married. He tried to make a go of gold prospecting, but his wife, Louisa Hearn, who had also done time with hard labour on numerous occasions at Fremantle Prison for disorderly conduct, vagrancy and running a brothel (the common fate of many poor women of the period), died at Southern Cross in 1893. She was probably the victim of one of the many typhoid epidemics that swept through the goldfields.

There is a poignant photograph of what was then called the Old Men's Depot, on Mounts Bay Road east of the Old Swan Brewery. Taken some time in the late 1800s, the photograph captures the depot building in the background, at the foot of Mount Eliza. In the foreground, a number of old men mill around or sit on benches and look at the river. It's a sad but tranquil scene, as many of the old men are ex-convicts, presumably institutionalised, seeing out their days on meagre charity. A quiet retirement at the Old Men's Depot doesn't appear to have interested Moondyne Joe, who escaped this institution as well upon being admitted there as an older man. By this point in his life Moondyne wasn't 'of a sound mind', and perhaps the Depot reminded him of Fremantle Prison.

Moondyne Joe ended his days in 1900 at the place where so many working-class women were incarcerated for so many years, the Fremantle Lunatic Asylum, just down the road from the Fremantle Prison. There were no friends or family at his funeral, and he was buried in a pauper's grave at Fremantle Cemetery that today carries the motif of a pair of handcuffs, broken free at the chain.

I remember skirting the southern approaches of the Swan River at night, sleepy and warm beside my brother and sister in the back seat of our mother's Volkswagen. The city across the water rose as cheerfully as the castle that bursts onto the screen before Disney movies, and I almost expected to see fireworks behind the cityscape as we crossed the Narrows Bridge, the patterned lights of the Swan Brewery depicting Captain Cook's glowing HMS *Endeavour* or a sparkly cruise ship.

Later, when I was a teenager fishing on the river at night, the lights of the city still flowed in motile beams of red and gold and blue over the dark water. Sometimes, while prawning in the various bays neck-deep, with the tintinnids' eerie chemical luminosity around my hands and feet, I'd look across to the city, and through my salt-smeary eyes I'd see the primary reds and greens of the illuminated buildings and sulphur-haloed freeway shimmering in colour. For a child of the suburbs, the city was never heard and it was never smelled; it was a purely visual experience, always out of reach. The fetor of the river and the silence of the night seemed to hold the city at bay in the distance.

Unlike in the bush, where the quiddity of things often startles and draws focus, there's something dreamlike about the city beside the stillness of the river, with its backdrop of scarp and bluff. Author Elizabeth Jolley pointed this out in an image of the quiet city in the morning stillness, where '[a]cross the wide saucer of water the city lies in repose as if painted on a pale curtain ... it has a quality of unreality as if no life with all the ensuing problems could unfold there.'

The mask that Perth shows the river has often concealed the true face of the city that lies behind. St Georges Terrace was once a street of famous views. It was the home of Government House, the dwellings of the gentry and the Palace Hotel, with what one Victorian commentator described as the 'world's most famous veranda', because of its view over Perth Water. The low rise that barely protected the inhabitants from the smell of the stewing, algae-heated waters of Mounts Bay can still be observed as a minor ridge that descends again as it approaches the Causeway. In Robert Drewe's novel *The Drowner*, the character Will describes this double city concealed behind the Terrace:

> Jostling his way through the crowds along a narrow footpath of oyster shells and sand, Will saw how the early planners had actually created two towns within the one. There was the lovely town comprising the elegant and wealthy St George's Terrace and Adelaide Terrace and their bisecting streets, with their macadamised road surfaces, Governor's mansion, river views, shady Cape lilac trees and stately commercial buildings and residences. And the three streets of hotels and shops and boarding houses and small businesses running behind them seemed bustling and prosperous, if only because of the narrowness of the limestone roadways.

Perhaps this is why Rodney Hall, in his late-1980s travel memoir *Home,* in a chapter dedicated to 'The Most Remote of Cities', was able to write that 'Perth people are friendly, this cannot be denied, and the pace is leisurely. Yet the city seems to have no heart, no shape, no character. In search of character, you should take the first available train to Fremantle.' By this point in the story of Perth, St Georges Terrace, which had once been, as a local architect noted, 'a street that you could spend your whole life on', had become the site of a row of largely featureless office blocks, symptomatic of a 'donut city', one empty of life in its centre. Although as Drewe's character Will suggests, there's always life behind the now glittering glass-walled facade.

The power and wealth of the corporations resident on St Georges Terrace was magnified due to the latest boom, although the landscape still changes dramatically away from the Terrace. In the narrower Hay, Murray and Wellington streets, there has always been a more diverse human traffic. Here, you could argue that the atmosphere hasn't changed much since the period described by Tim Winton in *Cloudstreet*:

Now the days were getting longer and the light was
lasting, he'd walk up Hay Street in the evenings
and hear the clock on the town hall toll the hour.
He liked to walk in the warm five o'clock breeze
better than the closepressed tram to the station.
People would be hurrying along the pavements,
calling, whistling, dropping things, skylarking.
Pretty women would be spilling out of Bairds and
Foys and Alberts. In Forrest Place, in the rank
shade of the GPO, old diggers sat bathing in the
breeze and swapping news pages. European fruit
sellers, Balts and Italians, would be haranguing
from the footpath with their sad faces weary as
unmade beds, and along Wellington Street trolley
buses would haul full loads of arms and legs up
the hill. The sky would be fading blue. The station
was sootrimmed and roaring with crowds.

The old diggers have gone from Forrest Place,
whose seats have now been taken by office workers
eating lunch or street kids with hard faces and sad
eyes, as have the greengrocers that once abutted
the now demolished Boans department store,
although their calls live on in the hawkers cries of
a bustling night market. Gone too are the desper-
ately poor who used to inhabit the lodging houses

and tenements of upper Hay and Murray streets, a stone's throw from Parliament House. Entire families would share single rooms, and balconies were walled off and converted into crammed flats. Under the advice of Perth City Council, these tenements were done away with and their occupants were pushed out north and east of the city. Initially they went to the equally crammed tenements of East Perth, and to some extent Northbridge, or what was then called variously Northline, North Perth, the Latin Quarter and Little Italy, due to its long tradition of housing new immigrants. In the 1960s they were moved further afield to the new satellite suburbs of Balga, Nollamara and Girrawheen, where much of the initial public housing stock remains, as well as enduring pockets of disadvantage.

While there were some luxury apartments along Adelaide Terrace in an area traditionally inhabited by the wealthy, the link between tenement living and poverty meant it was very hard to convince councils to build high-density flat and apartment complexes anywhere near the city. The resulting lack of a mixed residential population in the CBD is part of the reason why, on the surface at least, Perth appears to be a highly legible city, a term writer and polymath George Seddon used to describe the accessible experience of Rottnest Island, meaning that it 'can be easily comprehended, physically and intellectually'. Central Perth is a city of straight streets and right-angle turns that make getting around on foot relatively easy. There is little of the disorientation or social complexity experienced in a densely populated metropolis. Instead, as Alan Alexander indicates in his poem 'Capital City', '[b]y walking the streets I'm domesticated'. While domesticity of the kind Alexander is referring to here, one that suggests an uncomplicated happiness amid the 'cultural rub, the vin ordinaire' of the area behind the Terrace, is certainly not for those seeking edge and excitement, it does speak of the sense of remnant community that Alexander and many others found in the nearby streets during the 1980s.

Walking around the lanes and alleys behind the Terrace, it's pretty clear that there's a lot more happening at street level in Perth these days. This is primarily due to the zoning interventions of Perth's previous mayor, Lisa Scaffidi, the relaxing of once restrictive licensing laws, and the fact that, for the first time in my memory at least, a generation of twenty-something residents have chosen to focus their creative energies on Perth rather than London, Tokyo, Sydney or Melbourne. It's an observation supported by the recent statistic that Perth has proportionally the fastest-growing population of 25-to-29-year-olds in the country, by a factor of some 200 per cent, a majority of whom are choosing to live in inner-city areas.

Northbridge too has become a place that can repeatedly surprise, and for the same reasons. A residential area until well into the 1960s, Northbridge became home to a large Chinese, Greek and Italian population. Their presence is still strong in the many cafés and restaurants that thrived in the area, some of them converted from the original residential homes. Because the railway line separated the area from the CBD (although as of 2016 this changed), Northbridge has also been a beneficiary of neglect, protected from the wrecking balls of developers. A majority of its old buildings remain, as well as some of its sex shops and tattoo parlours, even if the sometimes sour heroin vibe that I remember from my teenage years has gone, as have many of the colourful characters who didn't fit in anywhere else in Perth.

Throughout the twentieth century, Northbridge was also the beneficiary of a strong prohibition market that saw the area become the centre of the city's vice and gaming economies. It began in the brothels on Roe Street and then later spread to William Street and the numerous gambling clubs around James Street, which were highly popular until Burswood Casino opened in the 1980s.

Of late the area feels rejuvenated, a result of the efforts of local government, business groups and artists to add texture to the once drab and empty Perth Cultural Centre precinct, in particular. The increasingly popular Winter Arts Season, the terrific Fringe World festival, the opening of numerous small bars and a general atmosphere of optimism about the place have added an extra layer over Northbridge's tabloid notoriety, the result of its sometimes problematic status as an 'entertainment precinct', the kind of place that thousands of weekend suburban partiers descend upon to drink, dance and sometimes fight.

My favourite images of the Northbridge streets were taken during the 1990s by Guy Vinciguerra. His photographs capture that characteristic Perth atmosphere of silence and space as well as the odd grace notes of absurdity at night: a vending machine marooned in the middle of a car park, or the eerily clean lines and fluoro-lit recesses of a highway overpass. He also chronicles those human traces of a disappearing community: the hard stern faces of an Italian family, flowerpots mounted high on a brick wall, the cheery smiles and vulnerable eyes of junkies and streetwalkers and street people.

The sense of nostalgia but also celebration in Vinciguerra's photographs is also a reminder that the truest, if most intangible, heritage of our city exists in our memories. The recent creation of a 'Lost Perth' community page on Facebook attracted more than 50000 'Likes' and four million individual views in its first week. A cavalcade of uploaded images soon followed, referencing all of those places and institutions now gone, including the old Perth markets on Wellington Street and the vast floors of Tom the Cheap and Boans, the latter with its 'largest showrooms in the Commonwealth' spread across two miles of carpet: a place of wonder to many children over the years. Something also obvious about the Lost Perth page and various other websites and blogs is that their generative emotion isn't only nostalgia for what has gone, but also naked delight in the daggy: the sense of pride in the way people have always made a little go a long way when it comes to entertaining themselves in Perth.

Artist Jon Tarry has explored this understanding that an emotional landscape ghosts the built environment of a city, even in the absence of the buildings, parks and places that once inspired it. His exhibition *In My Beginning is My End* followed the 2011 demolition of the Perth Entertainment Centre and the construction of its replacement, the newly minted Perth Arena.

Opened in 1974, the Entertainment Centre had a seating capacity of 8200 and was one of the largest purpose-built theatres in the world. Up until the late 1990s it was the venue of choice for stadium rock events, and many of my friends and I slept out front to get early tickets for the sell-out shows of acts such as David Bowie and Devo. It was quite a distinctive structure when new, although over the years it became tired-looking and under-utilised to the point that it lay dormant from 2002.

Tarry was given free access to photograph the demolition. Over the months he chronicled its progress, his Facebook page attraced more than 120 000 views as locals documented their shared history and memories associated with the space.

It's also worth mentioning that an open day for the Perth Arena attracted a crowd of 25 000 curious visitors, a degree of interest in a new building that seems unthinkable in other, larger cities.

Regardless of Perth's new urban charms, the vision of the city at night and its relation to the river still hold my attention – there is a harmony of perspective that has changed little over the years. The Mounts Bay waters that once lapped at the feet of the village may have been reclaimed and the foreshore gradually filled with dredging spoil, so that the river is now some considerable distance from the city, but at night this impression is ameliorated with the reflection of the vertical cityscape played across the broad level of Perth Water.

Against this watery canvas, the ferry that transports passengers from Barrack Street Jetty to South Perth moves like a swift water-beetle between the twin bridges of the Causeway and the Narrows. Traffic purls on the interchanges east and west of the city centre, with the long curling wave of the Darling Ranges and the limestone bluff of Mount Eliza forming dark cuffs around the centre of light.

The glittering faces of the St Georges Terrace skyscrapers tower above the older Georgian and

Victorian buildings of the Supreme Court and Government House, creating a layering effect. I suppose this is in keeping with the invisible layering beneath the river's surface as well as in the air above. Every second or third morning in winter, a thick inversion layer of foggy cool air many hundreds of metres deep sits over the land. In the river, for large parts of the year, the halocline system that sees freshwater flowing seawards over trapped pockets of deoxygenated saltwater in the deeper channels means that the shallower waters nearer the shore are the most highly oxygenated. The fresh and salt waters mixed there by the wind are best able to sustain life.

The hunting ground of Yellagonga's clan on the shallow and samphire-rich waters near Pelican Point and Midgegooroo's equivalent on the southern waters near Alfred Cove are largely unchanged, still home to bird species such as the banded stilt and hooded plover, but much of the area closest to the city has been modified. In the nineteenth century, when Perth was an important port on the river, dredging work facilitated boat traffic between Coode and Mends streets and Barrack Street and the Claisebrook Canal, and retaining walls were built to reduce flooding and erosion. Mounts Bay disappeared altogether beneath the freeway interchanges that lead to the Narrows Bridge, and the swampy flats that once constituted a few loose islands near the Causeway were consolidated into Heirisson Island. As a result of these changes, the black swan (*Cygnus atratus*) observed by de Vlamingh in 1697, the species that gave the river its name, and was still numerous when Stirling and Frazer surveyed the river in 1827, describing a flock of some 500 birds on the wing, is now rarely seen in numbers, although there's a large colony in the Peel inlet further south. The black swan is still reasonably common in the Manning Park wetlands south of Perth where I take my three children for walks. The children love its loud bugle when roused by the presence of dogs, or its soft crooning when comfortable paddling in the shallows.

The black swan was admired for its beauty and difference from its European counterpart, becoming one of the earliest symbols of antipodean singularity, but in the early years when food was scarce it was also readily eaten. As late as 1936, a recipe for 'Black Swan, Roasted or Baked' in *Mrs Beeton's Everyday Cookery* suggested that the bird should be cooked the same as goose: trussed, stuffed with mince and wrapped with bacon.

Prior to the building of the Narrows Bridge in 1958, bores drilled into the black alluvial mud on the river bottom discovered rich peaty deposits that revealed how deep the river channel was before the end of the last ice age. The walls of Mount Eliza flanked one side of a high gorge that flowed all the way out to what was then the river's mouth beside Rottnest Island, ending in the now submerged Perth Canyon, an incredible thousand metres deep. As recently as 6000 years ago, the river that has flowed the same course for sixty million years was thirty metres deeper in many places, but it gradually silted up as the water levels rose and the river became more estuarine.

Of late, the upper Swan and Canning are being treated much like an enormous fish tank. The authorities have added hatchery fish and prawns to maintain stocks, while oxygenation plants run bubbling black pipes along great stretches of the riverbed in an effort to sustain marine life when harmful algae becomes prevalent.

Stirling chose Perth as the capital from three prospective sites. The other two were Point Heathcote, which is located to the south-east of the city on Melville Water, and the port of Fremantle. As a navy man who had bombed American ports in the conflict of 1812, Stirling wanted a city that was away from the artillery-vulnerable coastline. The reports differ, but it appears that Stirling favoured Perth over Point Heathcote because of the ready availability of water. Mount Eliza also commanded a great position from which to potentially bombard the French, although as the settlers had already discovered, to their dismay, the rock bar at the river mouth prevented the entry of anything except lighters or dinghies.

One important early source of fresh water was Mardalup, which the Europeans called Clause Creek, after the navy surgeon aboard the HMS *Success*, F.R. Clause. It was later known as Claise Brook, and the surrounding area became Claisebrook and is now Claisebrook Cove. In many respects, the utility of what started as a freshwater stream, became a polluted drain and is now an artificial stream reflects the development of the city that grew alongside it. Mardalup was an important camp for the Whadjuk, a place where they could catch gilgies, ducks and swans and other bird species, especially in the adjacent Tea-Tree Lagoon, mentioned by the early settlers for its placid beauty and fringe of giant banksia and zamia palms. These palms, which botanist Charles Frazer described in 1827 as being ten metres high, are a very slow growing species. They generally add about one to two centimetres a year, which puts the trees Frazer observed at somewhere between 700 and a thousand years old.

Both the French and the English surveying parties used the creek to draw water. The English, I imagine, were particularly glad to find the fresh stream, after it took an exhausting two and a half days to drag their boat and supplies over the Heirisson Island mudflats. It was at Mardalup that Charles Frazer was confronted by three armed Whadjuk men and bluntly told to leave the area, although Stirling merely records in his journal that 'Mr Frazer discovered a freshwater lagoon, and I hit upon a Spring of delicious Water sufficient to supply all our wants.'

When Stirling returned two years later and chose Perth as the site for his capital, it was discovered that Claise Brook drained from a chain of lakes to the west of the site, reaching as far as

Lake Monger, and that the water table was very high. A similar freshwater source was discovered near where Spring Street in the CBD terminates today, and it was harnessed to power the colony's first mill. The Claisebrook area was used instead as an agricultural zone and as the site for the colony's first cemetery, on the high ground above the spring.

Henry Lawson wrote one of the first detailed descriptions of the Claisebrook area in 1896, after he arrived in Perth en route to the goldfields with his young wife, Bertha, on their honeymoon. Despite Lawson's status as a well-regarded writer, he and Bertha, who humped her own swag the twenty-three kilometres from Fremantle to Perth, were turned away from all the city's boarding houses and hotels. The Lawsons were forced to spend some nights sleeping beneath the Barrack Street Bridge by the railway tracks, before moving to the sanctioned campsite alongside Claise Brook that housed thousands in makeshift tents. Lawson tells the story of how a miner camped there was dissuaded from digging a well, seeing as how the land was fertilised by the blood and bone of the dead in the East Perth cemetery.

Shortly after, Claise Brook was turned into a

drain, to facilitate the easy movement of flood-waters, and a permanent abattoir was built on its banks. A mulberry farm came next, part of a failed attempt to establish a silk industry, and some of the area was turned into one of Perth's first parks. However, the coming of the railway and the establishment of the nearby East Perth Gas Works and the East Perth Power Station soon disturbed the location where the gentlemen and women of the nearby town might promenade and picnic.

East Perth was to become the city's main industrial area. The drain that still contained gilgies and the cove that contained plentiful crabs in the 1880s became an outlet for industrial effluent and a place to store the city's sewage before it was pumped under the river to the filter beds on Burswood Island, from where overflow was piped directly into the river.

By the 1980s, when much of the original industry and manufacturing had moved out to designated industrial areas such as Osborne Park in the north, the state government decided to redevelop the East Perth and Claisebrook area into a higher density residential and office zone.

Precipitated by state and federal funding, as part of the Building Better Cities Program, the redevelopment of roughly 150 hectares of inner-city land was at that time the largest urban renewal project undertaken in Australia. Enormous quantities of contaminated soil were removed. Today Claisebrook Cove is open to the river. Apartment buildings, public artworks and cafés line the banks that funnel into the meandering brick-lined spring rising up through East Perth, still draining off the water table from a catchment area of some fifteen square kilometres. My eleven-year-old son, Max, loves the bricked and limestone edges of the stream and the cement faux-turtle shells that enable him to practise his parkour skills. He leaps between the upright and levelled spaces, participating in a stream-leaping play that no doubt dates back millennia.

East Perth is no longer the industrial suburb it once was, with its overcrowded slums and wine saloons. Writer and filmmaker Stephen Kinnane, a descendent of the Miriwoong people of the East Kimberley region, describes the social history of the area as being erased by the 'neatly paved streets, faux Federation lighting, and three and or four-storey townhouses'. Kinnane's 2003 book *Shadow Lines* is one of my favourite narratives about Perth. Despite its often tragic subject matter, it illustrates in every sentence what Perth author and publisher Terri-ann White meant when she began her own narrative, *Finding Theodore and Brina*, with the words 'We learn landscape through love. The physical spaces and our own thresholds of pleasure merge and proffer all manner of things: sensations, stored expectations, moments with sharp edges.'

On the sharp edge of the curfew line, where after 1927 nightly police patrols were used to push out Aboriginal people still in the city after dark, East Perth was also home to many Nyungar and other Indigenous people who'd moved to Perth. Chief Protector of Aborigines A.O. Neville had the power to restrict Indigenous people's access to the CBD unless they carried a 'native pass' to prove that they were gainfully employed there.

Prior to the introduction of the pass laws, Perth had been a place, according to Kinnane,

> of meeting, of the crossing of railway lines, of rivers and creeks linked by corridors of black spaces. It was a place of alleys, of certain cafes and picture palaces that would serve Aboriginal people and others that would not. It was a town large enough to slip through if you had to, but small enough so that you could seek out your own kind.

This was a time when segregation of the races was taken very seriously. During World War II, a white woman in Perth was charged for merely talking in public with an African American. These kinds of cases, with their attendant rumours of miscegenation, were the staple fodder of *The Mirror* newspaper, but as Kinnane points out, the judge overseeing the charge made his point very strongly: '[t]he worst feature of this case is that people have seen you, a white woman, associating with a black soldier. If you are seen with a black man again you will go to prison.' *The Sunday Times* newspaper reported a similar case under the headline 'Women Talked to Negro'.

Amid this kind of absurdity, the emergence of the East Perth–based Coolbaroo League in 1947 appears nothing less than miraculous. The league was formed by two Yamatji returned servicemen, Jack and Bill Poland; a white returned serviceman, Geoff Harcus; and Helena Murphy from Port Hedland, whose progressive father Lawrence Clarke had formed the Euralian Club in 1934 to promote a similar culture of understanding and tolerance. With the support of Nyungar elders Bill Bodney, Thomas Bropho and Bertha Isaacs, together with younger activists Ronnie Kickett,

Manfred Corunna, George Abdullah and George Harwood, the league chose the Coolbaroo, or magpie (*kulbardi* in Nyungar), as its emblem, suggestive of both the 'mixed race' status of many of its members and the first notions of a creed of reconciliation between white and black.

Without the permission of the Native Affairs Department, the Coolbaroo League held the first Coolbaroo Club dances in the basement of the offices of the Modern Women's Club in central Perth (started by Katharine Susannah Prichard). However, because the building was within the curfew line, the dances were poorly attended. The next dances were held at the Pensioners Hall near the railway station in East Perth. The club, which was the subject of a documentary Kinnane made in 1996, soon became popular as a meeting place for progressive whites and Nyungar and other Indigenous people from across the state – many of whom were inmates released from the Moore River and Carrolup missions, where so many Stolen Generation children were taken. The league published a newspaper, the *Westralian Aborigine*, did its own fundraising and became a forerunner of many Aboriginal organisations that exist today. When the government finally rescinded the pass laws in 1954, the league was able to hold the club's dances in the centre of the city after dark – at the Perth Town Hall.

The fear of large numbers of Aboriginal people congregating in Perth goes right back to the first days of the settlement, when the dispersed and poorly armed colonists expected to be overrun at any moment. The fact that the Coolbaroo Club was able to continue operating for some fifteen years in this climate indicates how effectively the organisation allayed white community fears, while also maintaining its identity as an Aboriginal entity and thereby resisting the assimilating pressures of the day. The ethos that allowed for this survival can be found in the name of one of the club's regular musical acts, Kickett's Kustard Kreek Killers; it satirised and subverted the Ku Klux Klan and the racist beliefs that strongly existed at the time, but also channelled them into a vehicle that gave pleasure.

Although East Perth is still home to many Indigenous organisations, the bulk of the broader population moved into the suburbs. For Kinnane, who grew up in East Perth, what is lost is not so much the built environment but the fact that 'there was always someone to visit in old East Perth'.

69

Because Perth missed the gold rushes of Victoria and New South Wales in the 1850s and 1860s, there was never the concentration of workers in the inner-city suburbs that resulted in the 'workers barrack' terrace rows of inner Melbourne and Sydney. Perth's gold rush happened in the 1890s, and by then the preferred building material was the highly transportable and easily erected weatherboard. Houses sprang up in large numbers in Victoria Park and Subiaco, suburbs almost entirely populated by a generation of Victorians who stayed.

In the inner city of the mid-twentieth-century, you could still find weatherboard dwellings in Northbridge, West Perth and East Perth. There were pubs in downtown Perth such as the Ozone and Criterion; the Adelphi and the Palace and Esplanade hotels, each different in style and clientele; and for night owls there were jazz clubs and coffee clubs in the alleys that ran off Hay and Murray streets.

St Georges Terrace, while always the financial centre of the city, was then still home to a retail mix that included tobacconists, newsagents, sandwich bars and cafés in large numbers, mostly because the pre-modernist buildings incorporated a layer of floor space down a level from the street. I can imagine my mother, aged sixteen, buying her magazines and sandwiches from one of these stores on her way to work. My most treasured image of her is a black and white photograph taken by a newspaper photographer on St Georges Terrace in the early 1960s. Finally free of school, she's heading for her first day's work as a clerk in the clearing room of the National Bank, wearing a tight skirt and sleeveless white blouse. Her hair is cut short and her smile is unguarded, radiantly happy.

Her mother had made the snappy outfit, at a time when many people in Perth made their own clothes, grew their own vegetables, kept chickens and, like my mother's family, regularly harvested mussels and prawns from the river. Not only did my mother continue this 'making and making do' tradition by sewing and stitching many of our childhood clothes, she also cooked our jams and preserves, baked our bread, dried her own excess fruit on the tin roof of our house (the best dried figs in the world), and pickled her own olives. She also made her own cordials and bottled ginger beer, which would commonly blow up in summer out in our back shed. My mother remembers downtown Perth as a place of tearooms and jive joints and hole-in-the-wall Italian fruitshake stands, but also as a place filled with beautiful fabric shops and popular tailors and dressmakers.

Photographs of St Georges Terrace taken as recently as the 1940s depict a street of three-, four- and five-storey buildings whose continuous but divergent facades are packed along the footpath. There are few stepped, raised or recessed entrances, and yet the street has something of the flavour of a sketch by Dr Seuss: wild variations in building height and architectural style, plus the tendency to mask the buildings' brickwork with heavy stucco and concrete balusters, cornices and reeded columns, gothic arches and spires and mock battlements.

Much like contemporary corporate videos, paintings of the period tend to idealise the calm civic aspects of the Terrace, its 'European flavour', where a gentle light shines upon a serene vista of citizens at ease within the neat facades of High Victorian buildings. Architectural historian J.M. Freeland described the transition of the Terrace when he said that

[i]n 1892, Perth had been a primitive frontier
town with all the rawness and lack of style of a
pioneer settlement. By 1900, it had been dipped
bodily into a bucket of pure Victoriana and taken
out, dripping plaster and spiked with towers and
cupolas in a bewildering variety of shapes, to dry.

The Terrace might have looked 'European', and
therefore sophisticated, although one photograph taken in 1912, of the length of the Terrace
between William and Barrack streets, is perhaps
more revealing of the prevailing nature of the
street. The buildings appear eccentric with their
gingerbread brickwork and icing-white stucco
stained with coal smuts. The pedestrians in their
buggies and rickety automobiles are dressed like
workers, in shirtsleeves and boots and utilitarian
wide-brimmed hats. In this photograph the Terrace resembles what it actually was, a busy street
built with gold-rush money out of local materials
at the behest of mainly local businesses.

Perth's second mining boom began in the 1960s
with the lifting of the federal embargo on iron-ore
exports, and this immediately began to make its
mark on the built environment of St Georges Terrace in particular. The new-found confidence of a

'state on the move' saw a rush of new investment that required increased office space on the city's most prestigious street. In the majority of cases, this meant the complete replacement of the buildings of the fin-de-siècle Terrace with staid office blocks. In other cases, a compromise was sought. The 1971 Howlett and Bailey redevelopment of the Cloisters site retained the convict-built and Richard Roach Jewell–designed secondary school for Bishop Hale (the site of the original Hale School, which is now in Wembley Downs), with its Gothic arcading and Tudor embellishments and beautiful brickwork. It was integrated with the twenty-storey heights of Mount Newman House, with its splayed block columns and bronze anodised aluminium windows.

According to Jenny Gregory, by the 1980s approximately six per cent of the Terrace's older built fabric remained. This was primarily because most of the investment flooding into the city came from elsewhere, so development decisions about the suite of new buildings along the Terrace were made in London and Melbourne and Sydney and New York. These people would never live in Perth, and their decisions weren't guided by what was best for the broader cityscape and social fabric.

Instead they were guided by what was best for the bottom line – the downside of Perth's status as a branch office city. The situation wasn't helped in the 1980s by a Town Planning Committee on Perth City Council. According to academic and member of parliament Ian Alexander, who was on the committee at the time, it was dominated by people who had 'substantial declared interests in projects being considered by that committee'.

It's a well-documented and maddening fact that this period of opportunity during the 1980s was diminished by a brand of cowboy capitalism. As in many places around the world during the 1980s, this was a time of conspicuous consumption and punting on the stock market, but in Perth at least it was also a period of optimism and civic pride, especially after local tycoon Alan Bond bank-rolled Australia's successful America's Cup challenge in 1983. The win meant that the prestigious yacht race was held in the waters off Fremantle in 1987, and the state government embarked on a number of public infrastructure works in anticipation of the event. But Bond's wealth was ultimately revealed to be a house of cards, and his good friend Laurie Connell's Rothwells merchant bank (that had served its owner as a virtual ATM) failed despite a major bailout negotiated with state premier Brian Burke.

Like every city, Perth has its fair share of boosters and racketeers, although rapidly earned wealth combined with a provincial naïveté have perhaps attracted a larger number of hustlers in business suits than elsewhere. In any discussion of the policing, business and political culture of the 1970s and 1980s, there's a sense that it's precisely the city's noirish contrast between light and dark, plain sight and shadow, that reflects the way shady business was done and power exercised – or to use an old crime fiction cliché, the brighter the light, the deeper the shadow.

In 1982, author and poet Dorothy Hewett wrote that in the case of Perth, 'the corruption is partly hidden, the worm in the bud is secretive, and mainly bears only a silent witness'. Perth's aura of manufactured innocence, one that presents itself as 'naive, self-congratulatory and deeply conservative', was in fact the 'perfect field for corruption'. By the late 1980s, and the dealings that became known as WA Inc, the cronyism was very much out in the open. Bond and Connell were eventually imprisoned, and two consecutively serving premiers from both major parties,

Ray O'Connor and Brian Burke, were jailed.

Until the 1960s, you could argue that there had always been more sensitivity shown regarding the development of the CBD's built environment. This gentler transition and clearer line of evolution is perhaps best demonstrated in the delicate integration of the 1937 Art Deco Lawson Apartments just behind the Terrace, or in the 'New York skyscraper'-styled Art Deco Gledden Building on the edge of the Hay Street Mall, or the functional but eye-catching International-style Council House on the Terrace (which is truly beautiful at night, under multi-coloured lights). The spirit of the 1980s, on the other hand, is most clearly illustrated by the tower Alan Bond built on the site of the old Palace Hotel.

At the corner of St Georges Terrace and William Street stands what is now known as 108 St Georges Terrace and was previously Bankwest Tower and Bond Tower. It was actually the site of Perth's first licensed premises: the King's Head public house licensed to William Dixon in 1830. By the early 1970s, the buildings on the three other corners of the junction had been demolished, including the beautiful Donnybrook-stone AMP building and David Jones (formerly Foy and Gibson's, one of Perth's oldest department stores). The widespread belief that the Palace Hotel was next brought a surge of support from period experts; the 'Palace Guard', an organisation that claimed 23 000 members; the Builders Labourers Federation, who put a green ban on the site; and even for a while Alan Bond himself, who at that time was a city councillor and member of the town planning committee.

Photographs of the Palace, the 'last of the High Victorian Hotels in Australia', built in the Free Federation Classical style, show the lustre of its coral-white facade and tuck-pointed brickwork. It was conceived in 1894 by an American entrepreneur, John De Baun, and designed to be the last word in luxury. Its interior included imported mosaic tiles, marble fireplaces and Italian barroom flooring, and every single one of its bricks was imported by ship from Melbourne.

When Alan Bond bought the building from the Commonwealth Bank in 1978, he was granted permission to build his Bond Tower of fifty storeys 'consequent upon the retention of the Palace Hotel in perpetuity'. However, when Bond invited the R&I Bank, which was owned by the state government at a time when Brian Burke was premier, into a joint venture partnership to complete the tower, it was then decided that 'in order that the development be economically viable', the hotel needed to be demolished. The only exceptions were the facade and the foyer area, which now stand beneath the glass canopy of the tower.

Construction ended in 1988 and Bond occupied the top three floors of the high-rise, with the forty-ninth floor given over to a secure art gallery that housed Van Gogh's *Irises*. When things turned sour for Bond he sold his half-ownership of the tower back to the people for 108 million dollars and vacated his penthouse, leaving the top three floors of the building empty for nearly a decade. When Saracen Mineral Holdings vacated their lease to this part of the building in 2009, it was discovered that Bond's fiftieth-floor offices were still in their original condition, so that Bond's desk, chair and boardroom table were invitingly advertised as part of the new lease.

According to Jenny Gregory, the widespread opposition to the demolition of the Palace Hotel, the kind of redevelopment that was happening all over Australia at the time, needs to be seen in the context of what she describes as Perth's early awakening to the value of the city's heritage that went beyond colonial-era buildings such as The Deanery, The Cloisters and the old prison (now housed within the walls of the Western Australian Museum). Gregory believes that before the same kind of opposition to unconsidered development was harnessed in Sydney and Brisbane, Perth residents, under the auspices of the National Trust, were prepared to actively engage in protecting the heritage of their older twentieth-century buildings and river landscapes, though often unsuccessfully.

Public protest regarding heritage in Perth really began with the advocacy of the Royal Western Australia Historical Society and the formation of the National Trust in 1959, partly as a result of the threat to the Pensioner Barracks at the head of St Georges Terrace. This vast three-storey red-brick Tudor edifice was designed by Richard Roach Jewell to deliberately resemble a castle, with twin entrance towers and mock battlements and overt Christian symbology.

In the time of Governor Hampton, the barracks were built by convicts to house those members of the Pensioner Guards sent to guard them. Later, the great engineer C.Y. O'Connor had his offices there, where the Port of Fremantle, the Gold-fields Water Supply Scheme and the Mundaring

Weir were all designed. It became clear in the 1950s that the automobile-oriented Stephenson-Hepburn Plan for the Metropolitan Region, commissioned to outline Perth's development into the late twentieth-century, required the construction of the Mitchell Freeway, effectively bisecting the western end of the city; in turn, it became clear that the Barracks were likely to go.

The protest movement to save the Barracks came during the tenure of David Brand, Western Australia's longest-serving premier. His name is synonymous with the iron-ore boom and the mantra of progress, at a time when Perth's population jumped forty per cent in a decade. Like many Western Australian premiers, Brand was a moderate conservative who came from humble beginnings, educated to Year 7 level and brought up in the hardscrabble post-Depression years to identify with a core governmental role of attracting investment to the state. Together with his Minister for Industrial Development, Charles Court, another future premier and knight from a humble background (his father was a plumber), Brand established the Kwinana industrial area, sparked by the eighty-million-dollar Anglo-Iranian oil refinery and later the lifting of the federal government's iron-ore export embargo that had been in operation since 1938. Court and Brand also played a role in the development of the divisive bauxite and wood-chipping industries in the south-west.

Neither the Brand nor the Court governments, which ruled Western Australia almost uninterruptedly through the 1960s and 1970s, were particularly impressed by the counter-cultural change sweeping the world during the period. They sensed that the new-found wealth of the state and the rapid growth in population and employment were under threat from those who questioned unfettered development. There has long been a tradition of public protest in the city centred upon The Esplanade and Forrest Place, with the latter particularly remembered for Vietnam anti-war demonstrations and the literal rubbishing of Gough Whitlam with cans and tomatoes by angry farmers in 1974. There was a major riot during the Depression on St Georges Terrace involving thousands of unemployed protestors, and unionists and workers subsequently rallied on The Esplanade. Trade unionist Paddy Troy famously got around the bureaucratic restrictions limiting protest on The Esplanade by speaking from a boat in Perth Water.

It was in the context of increasing union militancy in the 1970s that Premier Court and his government introduced the notorious Section 54B to the *Western Australian Police Act*. According to Jenny Gregory, strikes within the Perth metropolitan area escalated from between twenty-five to thirty-three a year in the mid-1960s to 436 a year by 1982. Section 54B ruled that any 'crowd' of more than three people that gathered 'to discuss a matter of public interest must first have the written permission of the Police Commissioner'.

Such draconian measures to limit free speech and the right to protest were unnecessary in the less radicalised Perth of the mid-1960s. In part due to the success of the Brand Government's economic policies, particularly in a city that lacked a strong industrial or manufacturing base, it's probable that Perth wasn't ready for the kind of cultural reform instigated by a charismatic or flamboyant leader in the mould of a Don Dunstan or a Gough Whitlam, and perhaps still isn't. Which makes the metaphorical black eye that Brand sustained as a result of his plan to force the demolishment of the Barracks all the more remarkable.

In a rather Perth manner, perhaps, and one that reflected the strong links between conservative government and police enforcement throughout the Brand and Court years, in 1966 the police commissioner banned a planned motorised rally in support of the Barracks on the grounds that it would create traffic 'blockages' and 'disturb people in church'. As Jenny Gregory points out, this might have been Australia's first heritage rally. While the wings of the Barracks were ultimately removed, Brand then immediately referred to the need to pull down the remainder for the sake of 'the demands of the car'. When members of his own government voted with the opposition to withdraw the demolition order, he was humiliatingly forced to accede.

If the Barracks and the Palace Hotel protests defined the struggle to save 'Perth's soul' in the 1960s and 1970s respectively, it was the fight to stave off the redevelopment of the Old Swan Brewery that defined the generation of the 1980s. This was a far more complex dispute that brought to the fore the corruption of the WA Inc period, the issue of state versus federal responsibility for protecting sites of significant heritage, and, in particular, the newer discourse of Aboriginal land rights. My grandfather Ollie worked as a brewer at Swan for close to forty years, and the Emu Bitter

longnecks that my father drank when I was a child
– and that I liked to open every night with an Emu
Bitter bottle-opener – came from Ollie's generous
brewery allowance.

My mother remembers visiting the brewery as
a child with Ollie on Saturday mornings as he did
his rounds. She would stare at the huge copper
kettles that were two storeys tall, the stirring of
the vats with big paddles, the cold area with lagged
pipes on the walls (and the instructions never to
'touch the pipes as you wouldn't be able to remove
your fingers and if pulled your skin would come
off'). She followed her father up and down stairs
and ladders, to the lofts with the smell of the hops,
then over to the malt house across the road where
the original stables were, with the wooden kegs all
in rows on the ground level, and finally to the bot-
tling plant.

As an indication of the lack of industrialisation in Western Australia at the time, and as a
measure of the popularity of beer, it's worth
pointing out that in the early 1960s the Swan
Brewery was the state's single largest employer.
George Seddon described the Joseph John Talbot
Hobbs–designed industrial brewery as 'a latter-
day castle-on-the-Rhine', and generations of Perth

children delighted in the lights that flashed across the building's facade at night.

The Swan Brewery moved its operations first to the Emu Brewery around the corner on Spring Street in 1966 and then to Canning Vale in 1978 (and as of March 2013 to South Australia). The 'castle-on-the-Rhine' became an industrial ruin, set beside the increasingly busy Mounts Bay Road that tracks the broad river into the western suburbs. The site had been built upon and added to since 1838 when a steam-driven timber and flour mill operated there. It was subsequently used as a tannery and traveller's restaurant until Swan Brewery acquired it in 1877.

Friends of mine who managed to gain entry to the abandoned buildings during the 1980s recall the novelty of an industrial ruin in a peaceful riverside setting, but also the spookiness of the pitch-black darkness in some of the rooms, the knowledge that street people lodged there at night and an atmosphere of haunted silence.

The brewery originally drew its freshwater from the spring that emerges at the foot of Mount Eliza. It's still popular with people who come to fill drinking containers, believing that the water has healing properties. But the site of what is now called Kennedy's Fountain was originally Goon-inup, a campsite and ground of importance that the Whadjuk had used for millennia. For them it is a Nyitting (cold times), or dreaming, place, where the Wagyl, the serpent spirit who created the river, left the waters and ascended from the base of the limestone cliff up onto the area by the Pioneer Women's Memorial in what is now Kings Park.

Nyungar man Barry McGuire recently described the Kings Park area to me from across the river, at Point Heathcote, which is an early stage in the 'male ceremonies of coming into the Law' that includes another stage at the foot of Mount Eliza. Here, young men were housed in a cave of great importance to the Whadjuk people – now bricked over – until they'd learnt 'how to be within their community'. At Gooninup, stones of significance left by the Wagyl were maintained by the Whadjuk people, and sacred objects used in ceremonies were hidden in different places around the foot of the bluff.

Barry's father spoke English as a third language, after Nyungar and Italian, and while we stared across Melville Water, Barry sang the stories of the places around Kings Park in language, then translated gently into English. He finished with the story of Yellagonga, who was at his Goodenup campsite (now Spring Street) when his people first heard the European paddles coming up the river, 'whoosha-whoosha'. Barry told of the women ducking their heads in fear of the Wagyl, and only Yellagonga with the authority to stand on the riverbank and watch the newcomers arrive.

The importance of the Kings Park area is also something native-interpreter Francis Armstrong described in 1836, specifically the status of Gooninup as a ceremonial site and the home of the Wagyl's eggs. So it makes sense that when the brewery was put on the market in 1978, many Nyungar saw this as an opportunity to have the site returned to its traditional owners. Instead, entrepreneur Yosse Goldberg bought the buildings, which he sold on to the state government a few years later.

Goldberg didn't profit much from the deal, although he later made millions after Burke and the Minister for Minerals and Energy David Parker set him up to buy the Fremantle Gas and Coke Co and then sell it back to the government. Laurie Connell took his usual cut as a 'consultant'. During the WA Inc Royal Commission in the early 1990s, it was discovered that as a result of the sale, Brian Burke's 'Leadership Fund' had benefited to the tune of roughly half a million dollars in cash, some of which was kept in a calico bag in Burke's office.

When the state government revealed its plans for the Old Brewery site in 1986, there was a public outcry at its size and ambition, not to mention renewed Nyungar protest against redevelopment. The area was quickly registered under the state *Aboriginal Heritage Act* to prevent further work, and a protest camp was set up in the car park opposite the brewery, with large banners spread across the cliff-face of Mount Eliza. Supporters of the project pointed out that the brewery was built partly on reclaimed land and therefore couldn't affect the Nyitting site, while protestors wanted the land put aside for public use or returned to the Whadjuk people rather than have it fall into private hands.

A land rights protest in the heart of a modern city brought underlying tensions to the surface between so-called radical and moderate Nyungar leaders, between unions who supported the Nyungar and workers who wanted jobs, and between anthropologists who recognised the site's Indigenous heritage and the pre-Mabo legislation in place at a state and federal level. Although the state government was clearly bent on pushing the development through, the Hawke federal government initially vetoed the project after experts found the site to be deserving of permanent protection under the federal *Aboriginal and Torres Strait Islander Heritage Protection Act*.

It's not clear how the declaration of permanent protection under the Act was rescinded after the 1989 ALP state conference in Perth, with prime minister and ex-Perth boy Bob Hawke present, but shortly after the conference this is precisely what happened. Despite years of legal action, protests involving thousands of Indigenous and non-Indigenous citizens, union bans and mass arrests, the redevelopment ultimately went ahead.

The Old Brewery complex now boasts apartments, a micro-brewery and niche dining options that claim to offer a 'quintessential West Australian experience', whatever that means. I was overseas for the entirety of the brewery dispute, but even my fond memories of my beloved grandfather's stories – the characters who worked beside him over the years, the men lining up for their free middy of beer at every break, the challenges of keeping beer production going in a thirsty state – have been tempered by the stories of friends who protested and in some cases were arrested. There is now a subdued air over that once brightly lit section of the river that so entranced me as a child, and a sense of ambivalence that to me is unfortunately more suggestive of a 'quintessential West Australian experience'.

The expanded 'Old Brewery' still faces the Swan River, connected by a walkway to Kennedy's Fountain over the streaming traffic of Mounts Bay Road, and the diminished Barracks Arch still remains on the edge of the inner city, on a little cutaway at the head of St Georges Terrace. I suspect that the numerous people who don't know the Arch's longer story barely notice that it's there, but it's always a reminder to me of my childhood fascination with what I imagined were the remnants of a walled castle. It stands alongside the visual oddity of the 1939 First Church of Christ, Scientist building, which with its Deco lines, air of orphic mysticism and mausoleum solemnity used to remind me of the crypts of kings and queens I had seen in books, making me wonder who was interred there.

A short distance from the Church and the Arch lies London Court, a whole arcade dedicated to the Mock Tudor. My boyish imagination assumed London Court was a remnant of the medieval period, but it was built by mining tycoon Claude de Bernales in 1937. De Bernales was something of a tycoon's tycoon, even if he started with nothing and ended with little. Credited with keeping the worst effects of the Depression away from Western Australia, and by extension the rest of the country, de Bernales both perfected a technique to extract gold from low-grade ore and managed to convince the federal government to reward the production of gold, whose price was then at record levels, with a substantial bonus. The son of a Basque father, the grandly named Major Manuel Edgar Albo de Bernales, and an American mother, Claude de Bernales studied in Germany before emigrating to Western Australia in 1897, aged twenty-one. With a fiver in his pocket, he started up as a machinery salesman and repairman in the goldfields. He'd cycle from mine to mine with a clean collar and fresh shirt in reserve, slowly buying up leases with his savings. He purchased a couple of foundries and, ahead of his time, also bought badly indebted companies for peanuts. He understood, according to historian John Laurence, that these companies 'had such heavy overdrafts that the Bank of Western Australia could not afford to wipe them off their books'.

'Immaculate Claude', charismatic and handsome, introduced a touch of style into both the coarse mining game and staid Perth society, according to Ron Davidson. He certainly makes the modern mining CEO look like a bland corporate functionary, 'dressed grandly; [in] spats, suede gloves and a blue velvet cloak'. He lived in what is now the Cottesloe Civic Centre, with a sweeping view over the ocean. He was a notorious seducer, with mirrored panels in his bedroom, and was able to attract substantial European investment for his various enterprises. James Mitchell, state premier from 1919 to 1924 and 1930 to 1933, once requested that he not be allowed to remain alone with de Bernales, 'lest he sign away the state'. Like many flashy entrepreneurial types in Perth's history, de Bernales over stretched and came dramatically undone; however, unlike most of the city's other boom-bust merchants, de Bernales is still fondly remembered.

While London Court now seems somewhat cute, I was certainly captivated by the wares in the

shops of the closely packed 'medieval' alley. Like so
many children over the years, I waited expectantly
for the hour to chime, so that St George might
battle his dragon and the armoured knights might
begin their tournament above the clock. I wasn't
aware that the child-friendly scale of London
Court, with its statues of Sir Walter Raleigh and
Dick Whittington, its mini-replica of Big Ben, and
its plaster representations of unicorns and lions and
copper ships, was the result of an error. According
to Jenny Gregory, the Court was designed in Melbourne for a site 'that was assumed to be dimen-
sioned in feet, but was actually in links, so the
whole building had to be scaled down'. A link is
approximately two-thirds of a foot.

Further down the Terrace was the equally
appealing and vaguely Tudorish Government
House, where the Governor still resides. The Classical Revival–style building was constructed by
convicts during the tenure of Governor Hampton
and under the supervision of Colonel Edmund
Henderson, who also designed Fremantle Prison.
It is still set amid three acres of gardens. I liked to
look across from the Supreme Court Gardens and
admire in particular the capped turrets and gothic
arches, which gave the building a martial flavour,

although now I can also appreciate the bonded brickwork, the square mullioned windows and the views over the river. I used to imagine Hampton fuming inside, distracted by the exploits of Moon-dyne Joe, who was free from the hard labour of his convict peers laying down 'Hampton's cheeses', thick transverse cuts of jarrah used as road-building material throughout the colony.

Perth was very poor during Hampton's reign (because governors really did reign). It was so poor that Hampton gifted the city its first town hall, although like all civic projects during the period the work was done with convict labour. The land upon which it was built was near where Mrs Helen Dance had chopped into the first sheoak as part of the proclamation of the Foundation of Perth in 1829. Until the hall was completed in 1867, the area had remained an expanse of grey sand.

The Perth Town Hall was another building that caught my imagination as a child, with its medieval flavour and gothic touches, its Flemish bonded brickwork, its exposed jarrah beams inside. I was particularly attracted to it because of the traces left by the convicts, such as windows that were shaped like the broad arrows on the convict uniform. There was also the story that a hangman's noose was disguised in the face of the town hall clock; I looked eagerly, but was never able to find it.

When I was driven into the city as a child, I would observe the Barracks Arch and the First Church of Christ, Scientist before arriving at The Cloisters, London Court, Government House and finally the Town Hall. Each seemed ancient and culturally adrift from the city that had grown around it, making these landmark places in my childhood feel like relics left over from a calamity of some kind, and I suppose there are many who would hold this to be true. No doubt I would have appreciated the recent addition on the Terrace of the Christian de Vietri and Marcus Canning sculpture *Ascalon*: all eighteen metres of St George's seemingly diaphanous white silk cloak, billowing around the stainless steel lance thrust into the ground outside the 1888 cathedral named after him. From an adult's perspective, though, it's hard not to read the planted spear as yet another statement of violent possession.

After all, it wasn't far from St George's Cathedral that the corpse of Yagan's father, Midgegooroo, was hung from a tree on the Terrace for several days in 1833. He'd been executed by a firing squad in front of a cheering crowd, despite the fact that there were Europeans who identified with the Whadjuk and were curious about Nyungar culture.

There were many examples of friendship and curiosity in the period that equal the relationships portrayed in Kim Scott's depiction of the 'friendly frontier' at Albany in his 2010 novel *That Deadman Dance*. As Scott pointed out to me in a recent conversation, Perth also contains the largest number of Aboriginal place names of any Australian city (although not in the CBD), so that whether or not we're aware of it, Perth citizens use Nyungar words on a daily basis. It's evidence of the settlers' reliance upon Whadjuk people for navigation throughout the colony in the early days: it made far more sense for a European traveller wandering along the sandy tracks between homesteads to hail a party of Whadjuk people and ask directions to Wanneroo, for example, rather than North Beach.

According to one letter-writer to *The Perth Gazette* in 1836, there was no need for the government to employ an official interpreter, simply because there were 'many Europeans who can speak the native language fluently'. In some respects this was an intimate society, with Whadjuk adults and their children known to many colonists by name, and it can be assumed that the converse was equally true. However, the early familiarity also existed alongside a strong tradition of marginalising those white voices that considered the Whadjuk to be rightfully defending their territory from foreign invaders, or that demanded that they be afforded the same rights as any other.

Robert Menli Lyon, who arrived in the colony in 1829, was like many other male settlers both a Scot and an ex-soldier (although the details of his military service can't be verified). He was soon enough in trouble, as one of the few settlers who recognised that the official version of events under James Stirling's command was likely to be coloured by self-interest. Lyon made sure that his letters to Whitehall detailed what he saw as evidence of nepotism in the early years. He complained that all of the best land was allocated to Stirling and his military friends, who were indifferent absentee landlords (Stirling included), and that this was the main reason the colony was struggling to feed itself.

Lyon had been granted good land in the Upper Swan, but he had generously sold it to a late arrival to the colony and taken to life on the river as a boatman. He was a zealous Christian, and this, together with his admiration for Yagan as a new 'William Wallace', isolated him from the majority. The time of massacres was upon Perth, however. These were often blamed upon the 'lower orders', although it's clear that in many cases soldiers participated.

Even the urbane Irishman George Fletcher Moore, explorer, farmer and recorder of the Whadjuk language, but also the colony's judge, felt like taking up arms and putting them to use after he suffered the loss of some swine. He generally writes with affection for the Whadjuk people with whom he travelled on occasion and conversed in faltering Nyungar. However, this friendliness didn't temper the harsh sentences he gave different Nyungar men when they came before him in court.

Robert Menli Lyon put himself forward as peacemaker following the first arrest of Yagan, for the spearing murder of Erin Entwhistle. The man was a victim of payback after a servant on the same farm shot one of Yagan's friends for stealing potatoes. The murder of Entwhistle is significant because it also provides one of the first descriptions of the active role Nyungar women might play in their society. They had initially kept themselves away from Europeans, something thought to be a result of earlier depredations by sealers and whalers. Entwhistle hid his two sons under a nearby bed, from where they observed their father's murder. Yagan and Midgegooroo speared the prostrate man while 'a woman rather tall and wanting her front teeth, and who, I have been told by Midgegooroo himself is his wife, broke my father's legs and cut his head to pieces with an axe,' stated one of Entwhistle's sons, Ralph. The boys, now orphans, were forced to become beggars in the Perth streets, and the younger of the two, Enion, is said to have died of starvation.

The crime was serious, although for Yagan it was not a crime but an obligation. Lyon argued in the Perth courthouse that Yagan should be treated as a prisoner of war rather than as a common criminal, and he convinced the authorities to allow him to convert Yagan and thereby pacify the local Nyungar population. Yagan was clearly a physically and intellectually impressive character, able to joke with his jailers at the Roundhouse Prison in Fremantle before his exile to Carnac Island, south of Fremantle. There Lyon lived with Yagan for two months, and the Scot began compiling a vocabulary of the Nyungar language and the names of the clans and territories of the Perth area.

Made to wear western clothes and pray, Yagan chose to escape by dinghy – despite the fact that he'd only been in a boat once – and returned to Perth. When his brother Domjum was murdered in Fremantle, Yagan and his father fatally speared Tom and John Velvick on the Kelmscott-to-Fremantle track. The Velvick brothers, one of whom had been speared more than a hundred times, had a reputation earned when some Nyungar had come to the aid of a Muslim man, Samud Alil, after an unprovoked attack led by the drunken Velvicks and a group of about twenty other whites outside a Perth tavern. The assailants had then turned on the Nyungar and viciously beat them with wooden poles.

A price was put on the heads of Midgegooroo and Yagan. Midgegooroo was captured and executed without trial. Yagan, after travelling around Perth to solicit the advice of his many white friends, was betrayed by the young Keats brothers in the Upper Swan, one of whom shot him when his guard was down. He was decapitated and skinned of the distinctive cicatrice on his right shoulder and back. His head was taken to a nearby house where it was sketched by George

Fletcher Moore, who had earlier written in his diary that 'The truth is everyone wishes him taken but no-one likes to be his captor. There is something in his daring that one is forced to admire.'

Moore had suggested compensating the Whadjuk people for their loss of land and he knew Yagan personally. This didn't stop him making sketches of Yagan's severed head and, on hearing that another had claimed the head, writing in his diary that 'I should have been glad to get it myself.' The following day he made one of the strangest diary entries imaginable:

> I have rudely sketched this beautiful 'caput
> mortum' of Yagan. He wore a fine twisted cord
> round his forehead. I have been in a singular
> mood tonight, my thoughts running into or rather
> working in the manner of musical voluntaries.
> I sang one which gave me great pleasure by its
> strength, beauty and expression. Now, do not laugh
> at me for this …

Throughout the period, Robert Menli Lyon had been busy writing, complaining about attacks on Yellagonga and his people and about the idea of allocating rations to the Nyungar on a reserve outside of town. His rather Swiftian suggestion was that perhaps the real reason behind the reserve was so that Europeans could hunt the Nyungar at their leisure, in the equivalent of a game park.

After a number of massacres, according to historian Tom Austen, Lyon wrote directly to the Secretary of State for the Colonies, Lord Goderich, in London, and spoke to hostile audiences in the Perth streets, before and after massacres took place. At one gathering, writes historian Henry Reynolds, Lyon gave 'one of the most distinguished humanitarian speeches delivered in colonial Australia'. But it wasn't enough, and the hostility wore him down. Lyon left the colony in 1834. He moved to Mauritius, to take up a position lecturing in the humanities, and later to Sydney, although he continued writing about what he'd seen in Perth well into his seventies.

Yagan's statue stands before the city on Heirisson Island, surrounded by the shallow river. The current head looks oddly European on its elongated neck – the first two were cut off and stolen. Yagan lived his life beside and on the Swan River, where he learnt to swim and fish. His father's country, Beeliar, encompassed the southern side of the river from Fremantle through to the Canning River, although Yagan was ultimately murdered while seeking refuge in the Upper Swan, where for most of the year the river is narrow and quiet. The Upper Swan is also where Yagan was finally put to rest in 2010, after the retrieval of his skull from Everton Cemetery in north Liverpool, Britain, where it had been buried in a job-lot with a Māori head and an Egyptian mummy. Whadjuk elders led a private ceremony in the memorial park that now bears his name.

The Limestone Coast

The sight was now, therefore, anxiously strained
towards the shore in order that their eyes might
satisfy them and decide their ultimate fate. And
what did they see? A fine river, the verdant banks
of which refreshed their anxious gaze? No! Sand!
In every direction as far as their eyes could reach,
a brilliant white sand the children called snow and
wondered why the trees were green!

Jane Roberts, *Two Years at Sea*, 1829

Sand, everywhere. The same colour as the bleached
sky. A few diminutive settlers crouch in it, like
children at play. Mary Ann Friend's hand-coloured
lithograph 'View at Swan River', 'taken on the spot'
and drawn on stone, is the earliest surviving representation of the Swan River Colony produced by
a trained artist. She painted her husband Matthew
Curling Friend's encampment in March 1830,

soon after their arrival at the colony. The Friends, like everyone else, are camped on the beach or in the swales of the dunes.

Matthew Friend was captain of the *Wanstead*, moored in the Gage Roads channel off Fremantle, and the Friends spent only a few months in the colony. Perhaps because of Mary Ann's ready means of escape, her picture of the area initially feels light-hearted, not coloured by the gloom of others. Where colonists described their first impressions of the scene at Fremantle as one of 'complete wretchedness', Mary Ann wrote in her diary that it had a pretty appearance. The prevalence of white canvas tents made the settlement strongly resemble a 'Country Fair'.

Friend's perception was soon to change as the reality of her situation became apparent. Not only were the flies and mosquitoes and rats plentiful, the natives frightening, and the heat and hunger terrible, but she also hints at the troubles that were to come. She felt that Stirling had granted himself and his cronies the best land, and she feared that the colony would starve. She also mentions problems associated with a servant class who were no longer cowed, and the odd detail that because of the sand even Governor Stirling's beautiful wife

Ellen was getting around in her bare feet. Friend's complaints are always outweighed by her optimism, however, and her early descriptions of the landscape and the colonists' attempts at making do are entertaining, particularly their diet of kangaroo tart, parakeet pie, bush quail, and stewed and pickled samphire.

Friend's painting has the naive immediacy of a postcard. The tone is soft and the light gauzy, lacking the fierce blue that presages a blinding hot March day. In the middle distance, within the four corners of stunted and broken vegetation used to frame the campsite, a small clump of balga tree and zamia palm are sketched in the foreground, with what looks to be a dead tuart and live marri filling out the background corners. The stumps of severed trees are littered about, and the campsite consists of a couple of hoochies and lean-tos belonging to Friend's servants, as well as an odd cube that turns out to be the home of a horse that died of bruising on the journey over.

The 'horse house' (which Friend jokingly described as her 'cottage ornee') was also nearly lost, with two men inside it. During an attempt to bridge the rock bar at the river's mouth, the horse house had tumbled into the waves, drifting 'five miles above the town. Every time the men who were inside tried to reach the door it turned over. They were like squirrels in a cage.'

The idea that an ex-officer of the Royal Navy and his wife inhabited the equivalent of a horse float, and that in this they considered themselves lucky, was the message seized upon in Britain when the lithograph was reproduced for the wider public. This discouraged most potential settlers from migrating to Perth, as did mail from the colony that recounted the disastrous failure of Thomas Peel's settlement at Woodman Point, just south of Fremantle. Starvation and disease killed off one in eight of his colonists.

There are four people in the centre of the painting, one of them a young woman in a bonnet and long dress. All of them are huddled beneath the feathery shade of a juvenile sheoak, itself shaped by the prevailing winds. A boy is barely visible; he peeks from behind the trunk of the sheoak, shaded by both branch and fly as though afraid of the sun. The horse hut is a cube made of smaller cubes where the battens show through, alien in its linear geometry; everything else, including the settlers, is bent and crouched.

Only one man leans casually against a rail that

looks like salvage. He is the interesting figure, looking entirely at ease in his new environment. It is almost as though the painting is hinting at the temperament that will be required to feel comfortable in the new environment – the acceptance of the light and silence coming across the vast emptied spaces behind them. In this I think the painting functions as both ironic critique and optimistic portrait. The people in the composition appear marooned. Sand fills the foreground of the painting and the sky is sand-coloured, rising over them like a great pale wave. The trees in the new environment are unlike the trees at home, and most of them are already hacked down for firewood.

If Friend's sketch manages to capture any sense of optimism, this was a minority perspective. Time and again the early narratives refer to the sand as unexpected, and the tone of these descriptions is static – the settlers are waiting, doing time, bogged literally and metaphorically. Images of sand are used to suggest not only the infertility of the soil but also the failed pregnancy of the idea behind the colony. The biblical reference to building on the rock and not upon the sand was in the forefront of many minds.

The quartermaster of the HMS *Beagle* described

Fremantle as so insignificant that all of its sand could pass through an hourglass in the passage of a day, and even George Fletcher Moore, one of the colony's most energetic supporters, summed up his impression of the port town as a

> barren looking district of sandy coast; the shrubs
> cut down for firewood, the herbage trodden bare,
> a few wooden houses among ragged looking tents
> and contrivances for habitations, one poor hotel,
> a poor public house into which everyone crowded;
> our colonists a few cheerless, dissatisfied people
> with gloomy looks, plodding their way through the
> sand from hut to hut to drink grog and grumble
> out their discontents to each other.

This kind of negative characterisation of the nascent colony led to very bad press in Britain, best summed up in the sketch of the 'Flourishing State of the Swan River Thing'. The cartoon, published in England in 1830, captures the listlessness and despair of the hapless colonists over on the other side of the world. Five dishevelled and clearly depressed figures sprawl over on the sand before a jerry-built tavern and a shipwreck. They are glowering at one another, wondering what the hell went wrong.

The truth was just as alarming. The shipwreck in the background of the cartoon was that of the *Marquis of Anglesea*, which at that time was being used variously as the governor's residence and a storehouse. Later it became a prison hulk for colonists arrested for assault and disorder. It was under these conditions that architect and civil engineer Henry Reveley was instructed to build Perth's first civic structure: the Roundhouse Prison at Arthur Head. Like many buildings in Fremantle, its limestone walls were constructed from stone quarried on site. Reveley, who once saved Percy Shelley from drowning in Italy (but wasn't there to save him the next time), designed the prison to resemble a minor Benthamite panopticon, sitting solidly over the whalers tunnel that links Bathers Beach to the town.

I ride my bicycle most mornings past the Roundhouse Prison, where Nyungar men were held before being exiled to Rottnest Island. In 1834 the Pinjarup people crept nightly to the walls to whisper encouragement to their leader, Calyute, before his sentence of sixty lashes for stealing flour was carried out. Beside the bicycle track, somewhere in the soft white sand of the dunes beneath the prison walls, lie the remains of the first European legally executed in the colony: fifteen-year-old John Gavin, sentenced in 1844 to hang for murder. Gavin had been incarcerated at Parkhurst Reformatory on the Isle of Wight, but he and other boys were sent to the colony in 1842 in an effort to satisfy those agitating for convict labour. My four-year-old son, Luka, likes to watch the Roundhouse Prison cannon being fired (it happens at one o'clock every afternoon), although it's impossible for me to descend the steep limestone stairs back to the street without recalling Gavin's pitiful end, carried down the same stairs to the makeshift gallows.

Ironically the former prison offers the best view of Fremantle. On my most recent visit, I was carrying Luka on my shoulders through the old cells when I overheard an English tourist looking at a nineteenth-century panorama of the area, taken from Arthur Head. 'I didn't know it snowed in Perth,' she whispered to her husband, who joined her to peer at the photograph. While the image does look like the town is covered in drifts of snow, banked into every corner and gutter, it's actually the finest windblown sand, swept off the beaches by the southerly winds.

Once completed, the new Roundhouse Prison

was quickly put to use. In one year alone, according to historian Geoffrey Bolton, 'it was estimated that one quarter of the male population of Fremantle had been run in for drunkenness, and there was a good deal of petty theft and that was because people were pretty hard up'. This prevalence of crime wasn't something that diminished over the decades, either. Later in the nineteenth-century, the crime rate in Perth was said to be seven times greater than in Adelaide: the result of poverty and the high price of imported food.

Until hangings were taken from the streets, essentially because it was felt that the citizens' enjoyment of them was becoming unhealthy, capital punishment was a public spectacle. George Seddon describes the entire cohort of Perth Boys School taken out of class in 1847 to witness the hanging of convicted murderer James Malcolm. As was the usual practice, the execution was conducted on the site where the crime took place: 'The school was marched to witness the spectacle, which took place on the Guildford Road. When the boys were nearing the Causeway, they were overtaken by a cart carrying the condemned man sitting on his coffin.'

The medieval imagery is telling. Britain might

have been undergoing the greatest industrialisation seen in any country to that time, but in Perth the society of free men and women and their servants maintained many of the practices being phased out in England: the use of gibbeting and the stocks in punishment, serfdom for contracted workers, and a largely barter economy made necessary by an absolute reliance on agriculture and fishing.

The Swan River Colony was struggling, in part because the colonists hadn't yet learnt to read the land. That skill was something that came much later, when they discovered that the presence of certain kinds of trees indicated fertile soil. The open tuart forest that stretched along the coastline of Perth behind the first aeolian (shaped by the wind) limestone swale wasn't good soil, which was the reason most colonists clung to the riverbanks of the Swan and Canning, and then later the swamps that fill the gaps between the limestone ridges that rise inland. While on Carnac Island, Robert Menli Lyon recorded Yagan's description of the three long bands of geological formation running north-south along the lowland plain that in turn influence the surface vegetation. The three distinct bands were named by Yagan as firstly

Booyeembarra, or limestone country, characterised by tuart and balga tree; secondly *Gandoo*, or what is now known as the Bassendean Sands formation, characterised by jarrah and banksia woodlands; and finally *Warget*, the more fertile alluvial Pinjarra formation nearest to the Darling Scarp, with its marri, wandoo and flooded gum. This description of the landscape seemed to surprise Lyon, who felt that Yagan's understanding of 'the country will show that these savages are not destitute of geological knowledge'.

Lyon's surprise at the Whadjuk understanding of their country hints at the lost opportunities that were to follow, as the settlers went about effacing the knowledge of the Perth area that had taken millennia to develop. The situation in the first years was so desperate that Stirling sent the *Parmelia* to Java in 1829 for provisions, and later a government schooner went to Mauritius for resupply.

Perhaps the best that can be said of Perth's early failure to thrive is that it served as a lesson to subsequent colonisers. One of the colony's chief critics was Edward Gibbon Wakefield, an agitator for the model of 'systematic colonisation' that was soon to find expression in the settlement of Adelaide. Wakefield regarded the Perth model as an object lesson in how not to conceive a colony: mistakenly offering generous land grants to masters who would struggle to hold their servants and labourers when so much cheap land was available. The theme of Perth's difficulties was also taken up in *Das Kapital* by Karl Marx, who used the venture as an example of the need of capitalism to exploit all aspects of the means of production, especially labour, or otherwise fail.

One of the most common complaints in the colony was ophthalmia, an eye inflammation caused by Vitamin A deficiency. The only cure was a diet rich in vegetables and dairy products, largely unavailable due to the death of livestock (Mary Ann Friend observed the 'common' sight of dead cows on the windswept beaches) and the failure of local gardens to thrive without fertiliser in the limestone soil. Symptoms were described by one settler as 'agony beyond anything; a sensation of scalding water poured on the eyeballs'. The settlers called it 'sandy blight' and believed it was caused by the sudden transition from the milder conditions at home to those encountered on the bright beaches. A diet of dried meat, biscuit and beer meant increased sensitivity to the fierce coastal light and a corresponding night blindness.

Nothing reminds me of my Perth childhood in the days before skin-cancer awareness more than the blinding light at the beach on a hot summer's day. As a heavily freckled child with red hair and blue-green eyes, without sunglasses or a hat, I didn't stand a chance against the raking sun off the ocean, even when wearing that characteristic Perth squint and sheltering hand. But I was a water baby and always outdoors. One of the things that initially drew me to skindiving was the contrast between my blindness out of the water and the richness of colour to be found under the glittering surface. The neon green of the sea-lettuce and the olive kelp and sea-grass on the sandy beds within the limestone reefs were a balm to my eyes. I remember diving through the cool shadows under ledges where colourful wrasse and red-lipped morwong peered. I speared crayfish with my gidgee and carried them clacking above my head to the shore, one eye on the waves that scrolled in from the deeper water.

I spent so much of my childhood and teenage years underwater that it's not an exaggeration to say that, like Tim Winton, 'The sea got me through my adolescence.' Surfing and diving were an escape from boredom, but it was always more than that. As Winton writes, 'Freediving in the open ocean, for all the other things it is, is mostly a form of forgetting ... a stepping-aside from terrestrial problems to be absorbed in the long moment.'

We were nerveless kids, my friends and I, uncontaminated by the fear of sharks that for many Perth swimmers has suffused these past years with a sense of menace. The ocean may have been burnished with silver, but being absorbed in the long moment beneath the cool surface meant release from the hormonal confusion to be found back on land. It was also about the intensity of the experience and an awareness of what was in the water with me, beyond the crystal facets of the reef pools: the schools of herring flashing against the darker water, the numerous shipwrecks on the reefs further out. I knew there was a vast ship graveyard over near Rottnest Island. But nobody had told me that the dozens of ships were deliberately scuttled over the course of many years, having been retired from service. Nor had anyone told me that they didn't contain the souls of thousands of drowned sailors, an image that spoke to me of the transgression of the boundaries between solid and liquid, stone and water, land and sea — whose comingling is in fact a natural feature of the Perth environment.

Perth's windswept limestone coast is not generally considered a romantic landscape. Ron Davidson's witty and erudite 2007 book *Fremantle Impressions* contains a recent description of the fragile clarity of Perth's late afternoon light against the industrial structures that dot the harbour: the gantry cranes, derricks, hawsers and gas silos. The story, told by jockey and Melbourne Cup winner J.J. Miller to art dealer and ex-dockworker Larry Foley, concerns the initial impressions of the area by figurative painter Robert Dickerson. Dickerson was in the west on a painting expedition, and Miller invited him to the Fremantle beach to show him where racehorses used to train. 'Dickerson looks across at the tanks and pipes and industrial depots scattered among the North Fremantle dunes. "This is Jeffrey Smart country," he remarks to JJ, who gets the joke.'

The observation was made in jest, and yet there's

truth to it, in the light reflected by the shining steel of an industrial landscape and the aeolian limestone ribs that emerge from the coastal sands. There's that double effect of the scalpel-sharp light and the general impression of space and silence and stillness – the strange marriage of a realist vision with an absurdist tone. It's an atmosphere common to many first impressions of the city, and something exemplified in this passage from one of my favourite contemporary novels about Perth, Josephine Wilson's *Cusp*:

> In the parks and on the verges and in the front yards of suburbia, misdirected sprinklers stoically pumped black streams of rusty bore water out onto the sticky tarmac of Western Australian roads, sending steam up into the cloudless blue of yet another summer day. Willy-wagtails made the most of it, flicking their pert tails in the fine mist, while tiny black lizards darted for cover beneath a fragile head of blue hydrangeas.
>
> A fat bobtail woke from its stupor and sluggishly headed across Canning Highway into four lanes of oncoming traffic.
>
> … 'What was that? Did I hit a bump?'

Robert Drewe's historical novel *The Drowner* suggests a similar mix of the absurd and the sublime when his character Will declares that '[t]his is a landscape of such stark space and beauty that reason can only try to defy it.' There is a secretive side to Perth that has everything to do with this aura of openness and beauty; it's the feeling that the city doesn't reveal itself without effort, forcing us to look closer. Such a register of space and silence in a modern metropolis is unusual, perhaps, and yet my own sense of Perth as a child was that the city's spaces were rarely neutral.

Because my three children are relatively young, and because I spend so much time with them, it's natural that my experience of the city often revisits my experiences as a child. Down on the beach after sunset, I watch them settle as the colours on the horizon fade and they begin to sense the night's quiet ghosting, inhabiting the darkness in a way that's really only possible in a city like Perth. It's a landscape with presence, but balanced with an expansiveness that is perfectly suited to dreamers, especially those who draw nourishment from Drewe's 'stark space and beauty'.

The air is salty above the dunes that over the millennia have hardened into limestone hills upon which most Perth residents have built a home. But the air is also dry, and even the days of rain in winter are usually interspersed with hours of brilliant sunshine. Most winter storms come in the form of squalls that nip and sting and race over the land rather than settling in to drench. This is rust country, but of the creeping variety, and the fact that the atmosphere is most often dry means that abandoned buildings remain perfectly preserved, just like in the dehumidified desert interior.

The summer heat kills off the wild oats and other weeds that might intrude on the human landscape, and the paucity of water slows the growth of trees. It's rare that moss or mould takes hold on the bare walls of abandoned factories or industrial structures. It's this aridity and clarity of definition that reflects something essential of Perth, in the sense that what is built in this city feels strangely eternal when clothed in light.

One much-loved example of a building that stands relatively unmarked decades after its retirement is the South Fremantle Power Station, four kilometres south of Fremantle. When I was a child, the nearby industrial area was home to a foul-smelling tannery and an abattoir where teenage boys from Fremantle were employed straight after leaving school. (Many of the young women went to the Mills & Ware biscuit factory on South Terrace.)

The power station was built in the coastal dunes because the location was close to train lines carrying coal from Collie, south-west of Perth. Next to the power station was the old Robb Jetty, where the sheep and cattle driven from the stations in the hinterland arrived to be slaughtered at the abattoir. The cattle from the northern stations were forced to swim ashore to get rid of ticks; on occasions they broke free of their pens and stormed the streets of South Fremantle, posing a threat to children and the elderly, before being rounded up by mostly Aboriginal stockmen. The longevity of this cattle trade has been memorialised in an art-installation cattle run, made of steel, in the dunes near the power station. I go fishing there with my friend Mark and my eldest son, and to get to the beach we're forced to take the cattle run down from the car park.

The power station was commissioned in 1948, at a time when Perth's power shortages meant that electricity was rationed: one hour on, one hour off. From a distance, the towering stepped Art Deco structure can appear like either a Chernobyl ruin or a graceful remnant from a time when even industrial buildings had style. The building has been gutted of the gleaming turbines, boilers and tangles of pipes that once hummed with steam and fire, while vandals have knocked out the thousands of panelled windows. Somehow this dereliction only enhances the forlorn grandeur of the building for those passing by on the Old Mandurah Road.

On the day the power station closed, in July 1985, the workers, many of whom were housed in the nearby suburb of Hilton Park, described it as a 'happy place'. This was primarily because of its position by the ocean and its fifty-foot-high windows streaming with natural light. One technician, Ray Mydoe, who'd come out from England in 1950 to help install the turbines and worked right through until the station's closure, decided that he was now going to retire because 'I don't want to work anywhere else. This was the only place in the world for me.'

The abandoned station has been fenced off for many years, but that's never really worked to keep out the street artists, skateboarders, ravers and

homeless people. I've wandered the halls and balconies and stared out from the roof on a number
of occasions. Despite the growing sense of decay
inside, and the smell of urine, booze and rubbish,
I've always walked away feeling strangely uplifted
by my visit.

There are parts of the station that I don't enter,
namely the dark pungent rooms of the office section. These are beyond spooky, giving off a whiff
of danger that catches in my chest as I step quietly
over the rubble and broken glass in the corridors.
There are supposed to be bloodstained walls and
the remains of a crime scene in some of the pitch-
black rooms, one of a number of murders that are
rumoured to have taken place in the building over
the years.

I haven't been able to corroborate the stories of
suicide and bloodshed, although on a recent visit,
I was reminded again of the sense that Perth's
vital aspects are often concealed beneath either
a beguiling surface charm or a layer of unprom-
ising material. In this case, it's the barrier of a
fence-line that must be walked until an entrance
can be made, the facade of an industrial ruin, an
atmosphere of danger, and then the revelation of
entering the cavernous hall. The gentle sea breeze

catches in the tattered plastic scrims that once covered the cathedral-like windows, while the soft light plays over the hundreds of giant works of street art. There's a sense of being in a vast gallery, a basilica or a cave adorned with paintings whose meanings are long forgotten.

The power station has been used as a location in more than one film, notably Ron Elliott's 1998 Fremantle crime thriller *Justice*. With its cavernous halls, broken windows and fluorescent guts, it's one of the few interiors in the city that captures the run-down urban vibe so closely related to stories of crime and desperation. It was also used as a backdrop to American band Fear Factory's film clip for 'Cyberwaste' in 2004.

One other film that stages a violent scene inside the power station is the 2004 fight-film *Aussie Park Boyz*, which was written and directed by lead actor Nunzio la Bianca. This so-bad-that-it's-good self-funded effort didn't manage to secure a cinematic release in Australia but was a cult success overseas. In between set-piece brawls featuring rival ethnic gangs, the film lovingly details the Italian rituals of home life in the semi-industrial spiritual homeland of the Aussie Park Boyz, Osborne Park. While the power station,

Fremantle Prison and a grungy northern suburbs pub feel authentic as venues for la Bianca to display his macho prowess, not even his best efforts can redeem the film when the locations are moved outside. The story suffers a fatal decompression and all intensity vanishes. The characters appear like schoolchildren capering about on a film set, miniaturised by the vast empty background of silent bush and industrial light.

The 2009 feature *Two Fists, One Heart*, which its writer Rai Fazio based on his own experiences, had a similar theme of tough Italian Australian kids demanding respect, but it benefited from a bigger budget and superior acting. In its representation of outer Perth suburbia, all dry verges and sun-baked brick and tile, the migrant virtues of hard work and family manifest themselves in vegetable gardens and laden tables. The film manages to retain the integrity of its setting, in its depiction of both the suburbs as they are and the human scale of the relationships and the conflict. The fighting takes place *mano e mano*, and there is no attempt to make of Perth something that it isn't – big, dark and dangerous. Instead it focuses on the populated building sites and beaches and river, and the small clubs and busy footpaths of

Northbridge, before returning to the backyards and kitchens and empty streets of the suburbs.

Some sixty years after Mary Ann Friend painted her sketch of marooned settlers and wrote how 'we expected to find land but only found sand', and around the time 'sandgroper' came to describe Perth residents, tracking through the sand like the eponymous tunnelling grasshopper-like insect, men toiled in waist-deep water and near-total darkness some sixty feet below the surface of Fremantle Prison. These prisoners worked wet and barefoot in chains for six years to complete the series of tunnels designed to supply Fremantle residents with fresh drinking water. The first mining boom was on and the port town was thriving, although typhoid had become a problem. The prison had its own water source, but now it was thought necessary to construct a deeper reserve to store and distribute water to the town. The water was pumped to the surface by hand, a horrific job that left one man dead from exhaustion (this man's death in his twenties was recorded as being due to natural causes) and several others seriously injured.

It's possible to journey through these tunnels today, in imitation punts. The tunnels run north to south outside the eastern wall of the prison, roughly parallel to Hampton Road. As in all limestone caves, the air is odourless as the porous stone soaks up every smell, and the darkness is enveloping once head-torches are extinguished. It's interesting to spend a few minutes in this kind of darkness, where even looking with open eyes supplies no visual stimulus; the mind begins to involuntarily produce images, shapes that coalesce and drift, illuminated from within. It's easy to see why prisoners kept in this total darkness for longer than a few days went mad.

It was common enough for children of my generation to hunt out limestone caves with torches – and, if you were serious, helmets and overalls that wouldn't get snagged when you shimmied through tight entrances between adjoining caves. Some of these caves were engineered, such as those at Rottnest Island and at Buckland Hill in Mosman Park. Others were natural, caused by the slow dripping of a dilute carbolic acid over the years. The acid ate away the limestone but crystallised into stalactites and stalagmites the colour of wedding cake icing and the texture of the smooth whorls inside a sea shell. Just as they do in the tunnels beneath Fremantle Prison, the glittering roots of jarrah hang down, each hair on every delicate root holding a teardrop of water.

The roots work their way through the stone by secreting an acid drip that creates a tunnel of its own, allowing the root to follow. Often there are solution pipes caused by the roots of larger trees that have died and rotted away, forming glistering periscopes up through the stone to the bright surface. This is just as well, because the air in most caves is laden with carbon dioxide, and it's dangerous to be underground for longer than an hour. Once, as a teenager, in a giant cave some hundred feet below the surface, I crept away from my party and found a quiet chamber. I lay on my back, turned off my torch and felt the weight of the stone above me, the stillness of the air, the muffled sounds of my friends in the distance. I felt so comfortable that I fell asleep and my friends only found me after a frantic search. I've always felt as comfortable underground as I do beneath the surface of the water, a feeling of peace that has everything to do with the narrowing of stimulation to what can be seen, and felt on the skin, the focus on breath, the sensual loci of the body. Such moments in a cave really do feel, as in Nicholas Hasluck's poem 'Anchor', that you are wading 'knee-deep in darkness' and that the 'fragile ceiling is propped up by silence'. In the absence of stimulation you realise that the absence has a powerful presence: the weight of rock above you, the pressing of the darkness against your body, the air that hasn't been disturbed for millennia.

But my son Max, who is eleven and doesn't have the same history of caving, is unaccustomed to the absence of light as we work our way along the prison tunnel. As our fingers push off the chalky walls, it's like we're floating in darkness. Despite his excitement, he's also a little spooked, relieved when we near a small culvert in the tunnel and paddle over to where the others in the group are waiting. This culvert was where the guard sat on duty while the prisoners worked. At the end of the guard's shift, a wading prisoner would tow him to the exit ladder in a plated steel currach so he wouldn't get his feet wet. We shine our torch on a cement plaque on the wall. The inscription simply reads, 'Excavations for Fremantle water supply done by prison labour, June 1898, signed by ER Evans, warder.'

The plaque has little significance until you

learn the background story. Mr Evans was the warden who supervised the prisoners over six years of eight-hour days and six-day weeks. Once the tunnels were complete, he approached the superintendent of the prison and asked that he be allowed to acknowledge the work of the prisoners in some small way. After all, before the coming of water piped down from the Perth hills, this work had assured Fremantle residents of a supply of fresh drinking water into the future. Many of the men had ruined their lungs due to silicosis, or Potter's rot.

Evans was alone in wanting to record the labours of the men, however, and the superintendent refused his request. Undeterred, Evans risked his job, stole some cement from the prison stores and made the plaque himself, in the farthest corner of the farthest tunnel, twenty metres down in the stone. The plaque remained there in undisturbed darkness for some hundred years until its accidental discovery late last century. Evans' respect for the men is made explicit by the inscription. It's also telling that Evans signed his name as 'warder', a slang term for warden that points to the respect being reciprocal. It's the equivalent of a corrections officer today allowing himself to be called a screw.

I think it's fitting that the depth at which Evans made his forbidden plaque is precisely where the sedimentary limestone, characterised by shell and sea-urchin grit, touches upon the tamala limestone, whose aeolian origins are far more ancient. It is also where the water table sits, with minor variations depending upon the season. At this point the texture and porosity of the stone changes, becomes denser and smoother. It's like the difference between chalk and bone, consolidated by time and wind and leaching water – a combination of the elements that's suggestive of the broader surface landscape.

From an aeroplane, the plain on which Perth is built appears perfectly flat, but this false perspective changes at ground level. Just like the ocean from which the land emerges, whose broad-backed swells are most obvious from a position on the water, the stone hills roll in great westerly swells across the plain. These broad wave-sets of stone were shaped by the very same wind that sculpts the ocean into waves, ending in the ridge of Mount Eliza that's the westernmost point. There is continuity across the land and the sea, between stone and water. The swells of stone undulate in the same wavelike ridges out into the ocean, forming the north–south limestone reefs of the Parmelia and Success Banks – against which so many ships have been wrecked – ending with the line of Garden, Carnac and Rottnest islands, the continental shelf then dropping away.

Perth is one of the world's windiest cities. When it's still, you really notice it. The south-westerly Fremantle doctor sweeps off the ocean after the hot convection that pulses off the inland desert when the easterly blows. The salt in the wind settles on the land and the stunted coastal heath resembles the flowering seagrass that forms its sub-aqueous reflection across the sandy beaches, made of shell and the white grains of quartz and milky feldspar, carried down by the river from the scarp, deposited in siliceous blooms by longshore currents along the coastline.

Whenever I drive past the popular North Cottesloe beach, not far north of Fremantle, I'm always reminded of a friend of mine. After his girlfriend dumped him, he quit his job on a Sydney building site, packed enough to fit in a milk crate and struck out for Perth on his bicycle, an old thing that was ill-equipped for the 4000 kilometres of travails ahead. It was a picaresque journey with plenty of odd events and characters met along the way. On the Nullarbor he collapsed with sunstroke and was rescued by a passing truckie, who dropped him off at the next truck stop to rehydrate. From there he continued on, white sand and aquamarine shallows blocking out the creaking pedals and straining chain while the red desert and then stubbled dust horizons of the wheatbelt receded behind him. He rode into the city on a hot morning with the easterly at his back, cycled through the western suburbs, parked his bike, wandered down the beach and fell into the waves. As a cure for heartbreak, I am told, it was a total success.

The centrality of the beach to Perth's sense of itself is something of a cliché, but that's of no concern to the tens of thousands, often hundreds of thousands, who, like my friend, take to the waters to cheer themselves up. The sprawl of Perth is so great that it's approximately the same size as Tokyo or Los Angeles and many times the size of Greater London, and the length of the city on its north-south axis means that it contains many dozens of beaches. Every beach has its own personality and moods. Every beach is a focus for different communities who gather there to picnic and play and by turns stupefy themselves in the sun before invigorating their bodies in the cool water.

My own local, South Beach, is not as beautiful as the northern beaches in that the sand is a grey-white. It certainly has its charms, though, not the least being that it's walking distance from my fibro shack in South Fremantle. In the days when it was known as Brighton, it was also something of a resort. The early twentieth-century foreshore sustained a built environment that included a roller-skating rink, a picture theatre, a merry-go-round and a shark-proof swimming pool. The opening day of the Brighton summer season once attracted a crowd of 35 000 people.

Now it's just another beach. There is still a grassy foreshore behind dunes laced with islands of bonsai-looking Rottnest tea-tree, but it's on the sand that the crowds gather. Only the dogs are segregated, with their own beaches on either side of the main shoreline. Like every Perth beach, on summer days the water is clear and the sand is so hot underfoot that it can burn the skin. But unlike most Perth beaches, the swell is barely noticeable and it's rare to see the offshore pontoon pulling on its leash.

I can vividly remember the feeling of community I experienced as a child on the beach and also in the men's change-rooms along the coastline, showering with my brother and father. It struck me as remarkable that strangers in large numbers could be more at ease around one another while completely naked than when fully clothed. No status symbols or attempts at posturing. Easy conversation, earthy laughter, no shyness or awkward silence – something that I've only seen elsewhere in the *sento* of Japan, where public nudity has a longer tradition.

Perhaps I felt so comfortable in the beach environment because I was a member of what Robert Drewe has called the 'sand people', something that unfortunately had a lot to do with my complexion – and I still carry the tattooed inscriptions of Perth's sometimes venomous rays on my skin. As Drewe outlined in *The Shark Net* with a mix of fondness and revulsion the skin-peeling exploits of his own generation, it was still common enough for the Gen-X kids of my era to be permanently sunburnt for six months of the year. In winter my hair reverted from bleached wheat to carrot orange, and the colour of my constantly shedding skin faded to reveal a blotting of dark freckles that over the years coalesced into a pale tan. With eyes irritated by sand and wind, hair thick with salt, my friends and I would compete to see who could remove in a single ruby chip a perfect mould of the ends of our noses, or the twin jewelled scabs off the tops of our ears, or long sheets of papyrus skin off our shoulders and chests.

The beach has always been a place where people mix. The experience of warmth and light, cold and submersion, seems to sublimate the tribalism found inland into a pleasurable drowsiness or a physical charge brought on by the cool water, or a simple appreciation for the horizon of sky and sea, or even a tingling awareness of the presence of danger. Katharine Susannah Prichard's 1937 novel *Intimate Strangers* charts the effect of the dawning beach culture upon Perth's youth, as a place to literally and figuratively undress, and get away from the Protestant mores that regulated behaviour inland. Passages of stuffy dialogue that could have come directly from the diaries of the class-conscious settlers of the previous century contrast with the sensuality the main characters experience at the beach: 'It was one of those idle imperishable days of which there are so few in a lifetime. Greg was lit up by it, a little unsteady with sun-dozing, the surge of the sea, the youth and beauty of this girl he worshipped ...'

Sunlight unifies the characters in this novel

and illuminates their secrets. Prichard, like so many Perth writers after her, lovingly describes the effect of the sun setting over the ocean as it lights upon the domestic realm:

> Sunset, flame and amber, painted the edge of the sky: the islands were blotted dark against it: a hook of shags drifted inland. Windows of small wooden houses along the cliff took the blaze of the sunset as if they were on fire inside. Elodie watched the flame die in the sky, fade to saffron, and lie there in long flat streaks.

In Prichard's novel the domestic is integrated into the social, and the most persuasive of the characters is a handsome Italian fisherman, sun-lover, worker and fearless political agitator. This dark-skinned energetic swimmer moves easily between the different worlds, an outsider who stands in strong contrast to the insular suburban matrons and patrons who are blind to the effects of the developing economic storm.

Many of Tim Winton's characters are outsiders too. It's a reminder of the fact that for the greater part of the twentieth century Perth's beachside suburbs were often marginal places, despite the best efforts of the developers who parcelled up the land and sold it to young families who couldn't afford to buy near the train lines. There are some terrific photographs of motorbike races taking place in 1930s North Beach (precursors of the illegal Scarborough drags of the 1960s and 1970s), with cheering crowds holding their hats against the surging wind. The hills around are patched with jerry-built corrugated iron shacks, gimcrack garden beds, limestone streets, and dust clouds chasing the daredevil bikers, a visual reminder that to live by the coast in those days you either had to be poor or a real sun-lover. There was no train line and no tram, only irregular buses that drummed over the jarrah-plank roads, carrying locals and day-trippers and, increasingly, surfers.

My home suburb of South Fremantle feels most of all like a coastal village, a bit run-down and half-asleep, which is exactly how I like it. My house is built on loose beach sand, and only salt-tolerant plants such as pigface, cushion bush, dune sheoak and cockies tongue grow well. George Seddon wrote a beautiful piece about gardening in the limestone soils of his home a few hundred metres to the north. In it, he pointed out something else I love about Fremantle: the obvious harmony of perspective in a town whose buildings are largely built out of the stone on which they rest. Seddon's limestone home was built on a limestone hill halfway up to the rim of the stone chalice that encloses the port city. From the hillside you can still smell the salt and saltbush and baking limestone on the wind, the sound of ships entering the port with brute foghorn blasts, their flanks so high and wide that it looks like a wall of the city is scrolling back.

Recently I bodysurfed a huge swell at nearby Leighton Beach with my brother and our eldest sons. The swell was unexpected and we didn't have boards, but it was so powerful and the foam was so deep and the dumpings so violent that when we caught our waves the exhilaration was intense enough to remind us of being puny children again. We were riding the cold frothy banks of water as our father and mother had taught us, as my grandfather had taught my mother and her siblings while my grandmother, who never learnt to swim, waded in the shallows.

Calling himself a 'littoralist', Tim Winton has often captured the ocean's hyperreal brilliance, its importance to swimmers and surfers as a place of renewal, as a site where the possible is made visible, a place of meditation and forgetting, but often married to a sense of danger important to the rites of passage of so many Perth teenagers for so many years. Those immediately recognisable marginal characters who crop up in Winton's narratives of the coast, described in his memoir *Land's Edge* as those who 'feel forgotten, neglected, put upon, and yet proud to be far away, on the edge', and those ill-at-ease with encroaching suburban homogeneity, have been driven north, to the quasi-legal squatters camps and 'squat little towns with their fish-deco architecture' that dot the northern coastline. Yet the local beaches remain both a place of community and a place where it's possible, with a turn of the head, to 'have the mariner's sensation of being merely a speck'.

As a swimmer and surfer, I always preferred the northern beaches of Scarborough and Trigg in particular, where the limestone protrudes above the dunes and the waves are larger. Now that I have three young children, however, we rarely travel far to swim. We occasionally cross the river to Leighton or Cottesloe, where the white sand squeaks underfoot and the champagne foam in the shallows tingles the legs and fizzes over the shoreline and makes children giddy with delight. Mid-morning, before the sun passes overhead and shears off the ocean, the cirrus clouds above the horizon often resemble passages of perfect cursive script written in soft white lines against the bluest page. This is the picture of a Perth in harmony with the stillness and space and silence that is its truest personality, the only prick of drama being the spotter plane of the shark patrol crawling over the sky.

George Seddon, in *Swan Song*, describes a similar atmosphere in relation to Rottnest Island. For Seddon, Rottnest is the location that most fully realises the self-image of Perth's citizens as relaxed and egalitarian, tranquilised by sun and clean salt air, at ease with the pedestrian pace of the barefoot transition between shaded veranda and sun-bright beach, devoted to the simple pleasures of family, food and swimming. Calls to develop Rottnest with luxury accommodation are always met with resistance, just as proposals to build higher than a few storeys on the Perth coastline are regularly and decisively rejected. The beach is in this respect a sanctuary, defended as a timeless space, a place of memories and memories in the making.

The shark-spotter plane passes over my local beach in South Fremantle too, although like a dragonfly that has been hovering it soon quirts further south, where the beaches are whiter and the contrast of dark shape against white sand is clearer. Summer is the time of parties and barbecues, of breakfasts at outdoor café tables and drinks in beer gardens and pub courtyards. What draws many to my local beach is not its natural beauty but that it serves the same social function as the above. So many from my local community gather at the local beach to swim and sprawl and natter that it often has the atmosphere of a street party, an integration of the suburban park or urban space and private yard, a place where local people come together.

Fremantle is always a place where to walk down the street is to inevitably meet friends, but this experience is even more focused at the beach. At any one time half the kids from the local schools and their parents and grandparents might be present on the bank of grey-white sand, catching up and passing the time in easy conversation. With the heat and stupefaction and groups of friends lazing around, it feels as if we are somehow inhabiting a mirage outside of time, literally in the sense that the light is shimmering and distorted by the heat convection off the sand, and figuratively as an artist's mythic representation of what might define community in the coastal suburbs of Perth.

One of my favourite albums when I was a kid was Dave Warner's *Mug's Game*, which came out in 1978, when I was twelve. The record is a sometimes fond and sometimes savage piss-take of Perth in the 1970s, and I knew it word for word, especially the parts that related to the beach culture of local teenagers. The chorus of the thirteen-minute title track details the futile pleasures of Perth's night-life, while three monologues ridicule the city's inexplicably sexually appealing male stereotypes. It was the picture of the brain-dead surfie, Zongo, that resonated most:

A typical Australian beach, I'm struggling out of the surf, panting heavily for I'm overweight.
Two young nubile women on the beach:
'Oooh, isn't he spunky!'
'Which one? That one in the lurex?'
'No, not HIM!'
'That one over there with the earring in his ear and the bleached blonde hair.'
'That's Zongo, let's go over and talk to him.'

'Okay.'

'Hi Zongo!'

'Hi girls!'

'How are you, Zongo?'

'Far out!'

'What have you been doing with yourself lately, Zongo?'

'I've just been having an insane time ... Hey, look there's Rory! Rory couldn't get a wave if he tried!'

(*stupid laugh*)

'I've been having an insane time, last night I went out to the drive-ins to see Kung Fu Fighting and we drank two bottles of tequila and got really smashed. Insane!'

'Ohh, isn't he *spunky!*'

I was too young in the 70s to see Warner's band, From the Suburbs, but I saw him doing stand-up when I was in my mid-teens before he was banned for being too explicit.

I was also too young to see Perth's early punk bands The Scientists, The Victims, The Manikins and The Cheap Nasties, more's the pity. Chris Coughran and Niall Lucy's edited *Vagabond Holes* and Bleddyn Butcher's *Save What You Can: The Day of the Triffids* give a great picture of Perth's live music scene in the 70s and early 80s. Although it was limited to a few venues hosting original acts in 'cover band city', the scene produced luminaries such as Dom Mariani (The Stems), Martyn Casey (The Triffids, Nick Cave and the Bad Seeds, Grinderman), Dave Faulkner (Hoodoo Gurus), the Farriss brothers (INXS), the Snarski brothers Mark (Chad's Tree) and Rob (Chad's Tree, The Black-eyed Susans), David McComb, Robert McComb, Alsy MacDonald and Jill Birt (The Triffids), Kim Salmon (The Scientists, Beasts of Bourbon) and the legendary drummer James Baker (The Scientists, Hoodoo Gurus, Beasts of Bourbon).

It wasn't until I was living in London in my late teens that I heard either The Scientists or The Triffids, played to me by an Irish friend. He knew I was into The Birthday Party and The Pop Group, which seemed to suit the ambience of our grimy Wandsworth squat. While I immediately loved the swampy sounds of The Scientists, I'll never forget the first time I heard The Triffids' 'Estuary Bed'. Reminded of the limestone coast that I'd abandoned, I think it was the first time I ever experienced nostalgia, and it was certainly the first moment I felt a twinge of longing for home. Hearing the descriptions of my Perth childhood captured so quietly, I wondered if perhaps my 'old skin' wasn't shed after all.

When I look back on it, listening to The Triffids' album *Born Sandy Devotional* for the first time was also something of a 'growing up' moment for me, aged nineteen on the other side of the planet. It triggered a new awareness that ambivalence might be turned into something other than ridicule – into art, in this case. The sound was, as described by Butcher, 'both spacious and claustrophobic', exactly how I'd felt as a teenager in a city where it seemed that the brightness was always turned up but the volume turned down. As Niall Lucy asked, how *had* The Triffids managed to overcome the problem of all Perth artists, whatever the form, that is, 'how to lower your voice and still be heard above the noise?' Perhaps, I wondered, by tuning into the ambivalence made explicit in the promo video for their song 'Spanish Blue', with its imagery of hanging out and mucking around that had a clear undercurrent of restlessness: 'Nothing happens here, nothing gets done, but you get to like it, you get to like the beating of the sun, the washing of the sun ...' The Triffids' frontman David McComb later suggested something of the sort in an interview with Lucy when he claimed that 'I find no emotion real, in any art form, unless it's present with its opposite.'

It wasn't only ambivalence but also a sense of possibility that made me leave Perth. After that first pang of homesickness, I wondered whether my mixed feelings about my hometown might one day lead to my return (after ten years mostly bumming around, as it turned out). As a teenager who'd lived in more places across four different continents than I'd experienced years on the planet, I wondered whether a home that suggested itself in an art of contradictions, drawn to the darkness on the edge of town but also the fragile clarity of a child's feelings, was something that I needed more than noise, crowds and concrete.

From the late 1980s, with the break-up of The Stems and The Triffids, it was no surprise to see a new generation turn Perth's isolation and lack of expectation into a freedom to experiment and develop organically, channelling a lack of ready culture into the necessity to create their own. This is true of all Perth art forms, but it's perhaps most obvious in the success of its musicians. Plenty of acts over the past twenty years have gone on to national – and often international – success, often without having to leave their Perth base: Ammonia,

Jebediah, The John Butler Trio, Eskimo Joe, Little Birdy, The Sleepy Jackson, The Panics, Kill Devil Hills, Gyroscope, Karnivool, The Drones, Stella Donnelly, Troy Sivan, Birds of Tokyo, Schvendes, Pendulum and more recently Abbe May, Drapht, San Cisco, Pond and Tame Impala (I could go on).

It means a lot, of course, to have local culture that speaks to your own place and your own time. At a recent party on a warm summer evening, a woman sitting next to me mentioned how during the latest heatwave she'd taken to going to bed early, lying beneath her ceiling fan, and listening to The Triffids' *Born Sandy Devotional* and *The Black Swan* over and over again, in particular the song 'Too Hot to Move, Too Hot to Think', both as a panacea and a reminder that tenderness has been found, even in the sometimes brutal summer heat.

Robert Drewe's short story 'The Water Person and the Tree Person' expresses something of the way I feel about the limestone coast of Perth, its importance to a sense of place and civic identity. Part of Drewe's broad thesis is that to be a Perth child is to develop an awareness of the natural world that verges on the uncanny, imparted by osmosis as much as by teaching and learning. The main character, Andy Melrose, feels as though his wife is belittling him by stating that he is a water person while she is a tree person. Melrose, as a product of a state whose key economic indicators at the time are 'timber and whaling and asbestos', feels increasingly distanced from his wife, 'product of a middle-class Melbourne garden suburb of autumnal tones ... and the manicured cold-weather flora of Europe'. Although the couple live in Perth, she is an academic whose urbane friends ridicule his daily swim and suspiciously 'manly' ability to change a car tyre. He can't help feeling defensive about the fact that he's a product of his environment, just as she is of hers:

> What did she expect? Unlike her, he'd grown up on this limestone coast, with the roaring forties blowing sand into his ears and the smell of estuary algae in his nostrils every night as he fell asleep. Ever since, the landscape in his mind's eye was a crumbly moonscape of a coastline, a glaring beached desert fringed by those two big and wondrous oases, the Swan River and the Indian Ocean.

Melrose suspects that his wife's love of the bush is just 'literary-political correctness', a fictional landscape of the denatured urban mind, while his is a sense of attachment felt in the body.

The limestone coast has its freedoms but also its dangers, and my local beach is not all peace and light. I once witnessed a brawl that involved upwards of fifty people, the result of a family feud, and there is occasionally violent drunkenness in the evenings. Homeless men and women used to sleep in the hollows within the acacia, melaleuca and hakea bushes that cover the dunes, and parents don't let their children stray there. Mark Reid's poem 'Ode to South Beach' captures the beach's sometimes mood of sulkiness and decay when he describes its 'miserly west coast wash' and 'rabbity scrub' as he walks the dog:

> I am walking the dog beach, old Manners
> arse up snout down on the trail
> of vermin or the corpses of sea creatures.
> I am giddy with aroma, brine,
> the stench of pickled things tossed
> from the ocean's window.

There is a Shaun Tan painting that perfectly catches this beachside id, beyond the usual depictions of its beauty and significance to local swimmers, walkers, surfers and multitude 'fools on the hill' – the focus on the jade-coloured reefs and the cobalt waters and volcanic sunsets. In Tan's *North Beach*, only a sliver of brilliant blue ocean is visible, hemmed in on all sides by groynes covered in the 'pickled things' of Reid's poem, set against a human-sculpted vertical bank and a darkened snip of sky. There are railings and stairs and road signs, powerlines and grey concrete buildings. The constructed overwhelms the natural. There is none of the space and comfort we associate with the beach – a few limestone bones that I always connect with the northern beaches poke through but most have been concreted over. A lone swimmer dries himself with a towel, facing inland, in line with the unusual perspective of the painting, a place where the light is muted and the perspective diminished.

A second Shaun Tan painting, *West Coast Highway*, reinforces the theme of *North Beach*. There is the same absence of people, the same fragment of ocean tucked in a corner behind a foreground almost completely carpeted with bitumen, the same tired-looking coastal heath and a muted grey sky. The same signs and railings and kerbs and powerlines. The ubiquitous burn-outs feature this time, black smears of carbonised rubber. And yet the light is gentle and the mood is unmistakably Perth. The light and the absence of people give the painting an eternal quality. There are no weeds; there is nothing to disturb the picture going forward into time. Watching the Oscar-winning animated short film *The Lost Thing*, based on Tan's story of the same name, I was struck by how much the setting, despite its fantastical imagery, reminded me of Perth.

Tan now lives in Melbourne, but there is something about his paintings of suburban life that expresses my own childhood in the suburbs of Perth. Perhaps it's the children negotiating the quietness and stillness of empty streets and parks and paths, always illuminated and crisply alive, even when the lines are blurred and the theme is darker. There is one picture in particular: 'Our Expedition: Cliff' from Tan's book *Tales from Outer Suburbia*. In this pastel crayon drawing there is no natural environment left at all. Manicured suburbia stretches right to the limits of the vertical cliff edge, which is itself constructed of large blocks, above the level of the clouds. The light is warm and generous, and the shadows of the two children who sit comfortably on the edge of the world are long. It's the kind of light that's often a relief after the fierce light of a hot summer's day. It brings out the best in the Perth landscape, just as the soft clear light and clean air of winter brings Perth into the crispest focus, drawing out all of the colours and textures of a cityscape usually bleached by the sun. Concrete pipes pour waste out into the sky, birds hover at the children's feet. Fences, signs, powerlines. The children are confident, at ease; they are observing their world, much like the sole young man in Mary Ann Friend's painting some 180 years earlier, gazing hopefully out into the future. The children each carry a small knapsack. They too are on an expedition, set down at the edge of the world, but there is no sign that they feel thwarted.

On warm nights when the sea breeze is gentle, my son Max and I wait in the car park at our local beach for the sunset to fade from glossy red to a faint saffron glaze over the ocean horizon. On other nights the sunset mingles all the gaudy colours of a fruit bowl, a canvas of blood orange and tangerine zest, fading to a thin watermelon red, leaving a lemony haze in its wake. On other occasions the sunset captures the alchemical drama of a blacksmith's workshop, all fire and heat and steam as the glowing orb submerges in water, giving off an angry crimson mist that hangs in the air for nearly an hour. It's hard to do justice to the sunsets over the Indian Ocean with words, although many have tried. The first example I'm aware of was written by a painter, Louisa Clifton, in March 1840:

> The colouring as the sun began to decline became exquisitely soft and radiant, the hills robed in the brightest lakes and blues, the sky reflecting every colour in the rainbow, and yet so softly that every tint completely melted into one another. I cannot easily cease to remember the first Australian sunset.

It's at this point that my son and I don our old sandshoes and check our gidgees, waiting until the beach is empty before we enter the water in the final moments of dusk. The ocean takes on a slippery celluloid quality, as it does just before dawn, when like a darkroom image coming into focus the murky shapes beneath the surface become distinct, stray photons illuminating the water from within, the sun not yet on the eastern horizon. It was then that my friends and I used to enter the water to go spear-fishing, having ached through the sleepless night with the special excitement that was reserved for dawn surfing, or dawn skin-diving. There would be insufficient light to see by and only the cheering sound of my friend Fergus singing through his snorkel, his breathing rapid with the cold and dread of the darker water ahead, coming slowly into light.

Max and I turn on our torches and begin to mark the catfish, or cobbler as they're locally known, that are already at the waterline, bowled over by the bigger waves but nosing into the shallows to feed. By day secretive and hidden in the weed-beds, by night the cobbler are fearless, often stranded on the beach between waves. They swim between our legs, their slimy skin always sending a bolt of shock though me. Unlike Max, who so far has been lucky, I know how painful it is to step on the cobbler's barbs, and the memory of the fierce agony can be felt from my toes to my fingertips. We wade through the chop looking for a single large fish for the plate. As much as anything the hunt is an exercise in teaching my son patience and restraint – fathers having taught their sons to gidgee catfish in this area and in roughly the same fashion for tens of thousands of years. Finally, we see the broad sandy flank and swirly ribbons of a larger fish and the spear is sent home.

Max beheads and guts the fish while I watch over the ocean: the sulphur lights of the port to my right, the winking lights marking the Gage Roads channel further out, the bright caustic bloom over Kwinana to the south. The suburbs there are named after settler ships: Parmelia, Rockingham, Success, Orelia, Medina. This is the season for shark attacks, and despite the fact that I made peace with my fear of them long ago, I am strangely unsettled by a recent article in the paper that described a twenty-foot tagged female white pointer cruising longshore through the night, from Safety Bay in the south to Quinns Rocks in the north, back and forth, down and back.

Further south is where I fish with my friend Mark. We've been fishing here for years, more for the company and sunset than the catch. Sometimes the tailor are on, sometimes skippy and tarwhine and always herring. For a while there we caught and released an old Port Jackson shark every time we cast a line. Once a great black seal the size of a small car waddled up behind my back, so that when

I turned it was waiting with big friendly eyes. It sat and watched us for a while before surfing off into the waves. Our tradition is to always put the first fish back, because of some forgotten superstition, no matter that on occasions it's the only fish for the night. Something that adds emotional weight to this superstition is the bronze statue that stands in the waves: a horseman turning his blank face over his shoulder, casting his eyes back to the port where his wife and children lie sleeping, his horse raising its head in fear.

Tony Jones's statue memorialising the engineer C.Y. O'Connor is my favourite in Perth, despite the tragic subject matter. The statue is part of the living environment rather than a static image lodged in a public place, and its horseman sits stirrup deep or soused to the neck depending on the tide. He rides in the waves at roughly the place where on the morning of 10 March 1902 O'Connor removed and pocketed his dentures before he put the barrel of a .38 revolver into his mouth and pulled the trigger.

The statue is just out of our casting range, although it sits there in the darkness, catching the blinking illumination of the channel markers. One night at a nearby beachside rave I stripped down and swam out to have a closer look. The moonlight illuminated the horse's flared nostrils and panicked eyes, animated by confusion and fear of the gunshot, while the horseman faces the port perfectly calm, expressionless – he is already at peace, on his way elsewhere. Once a year, on his birthday, O'Connor's descendents swim out to the statue and perform a small private ceremony while sprinkling bougainvillea flowers and treading water, much like surfers do to celebrate the lives of their shark-eaten friends, at the very location where blood mingled with water.

O'Connor's body was found by a boy next to the Robb Jetty site and what is now the remains of the scuttled *Wyola*. The boy worked in the nearby lime kilns and raised the alarm. By the time help arrived in the form of the local constabulary the body had drifted into deeper water, from where it was retrieved. In her short story 'The Prospect of Grace', Amanda Curtin describes how 'Constable Honner recovered the body and examined the scene, reporting that O'Connor's horse had entered the water at a canter. The tracks came out again near the jetty, which was splashed with wet sand "as if the horse had got a fright." There were no footprints.'

O'Connor was the son of Irish parents who'd sold their farm during the potato famine to feed starving locals, and he retained a strong Irish accent to the end. He was widely revered in Perth as the man who not only created the modern port of Fremantle, which is still functioning effectively after more than a century of use, but also brought water to Perth after the creation of the dams and weirs in the catchments of the Helena River. Most ambitious of all was O'Connor's engineering of the pipeline that carried water across the desert to Coolgardie/Kalgoorlie, to an inland community where water was more expensive than beer, across 600 kilometres of country with a daytime temperature range of 0°C to 50°C. The Coolgardie pipeline was an unrivalled feat of engineering for the time, although O'Connor didn't live to see its completion.

A tragic figure, O'Connor is a subject made for literary representation. Drewe describes his mythic qualities in *The Drowner*:

> The Chief is a formidable sight cantering on his grey hunter out of the dawn mist. Through the shallows and across the spit, scattering swans before him. A thin and straight-backed six-footer,

all his control coming from his hips, the early
sunrays shooting off his spray, he looks something
of a centaur.

O'Connor was a tall and lanky man with a grey
beard, strong nose and heavy black eyebrows. His
darkly intelligent eyes were set in a kindly face.
Premier John Forrest headhunted him from a
posting in New Zealand and made him chief engineer whose purview included 'harbours, railways,
everything'. His was a well-paid public servant's
position that coincided with a time when the
colonial government finally had the energy and
means to commence major infrastructure works.
O'Connor's daughter Kathleen, one of the progen-
itors of modernist painting in Australia, said that
her father was such a hard worker and so absorbed
in his various projects that he barely realised
they'd moved countries.

In John Forrest, O'Connor had an equally
energetic premier beside him. If Forrest had been
born in the eastern states, he would be far better
known as an explorer and surveyor, along with
his reputation as one of the fathers of Federation.
As a younger man he had explored some of the
remotest desert points in the Western Australian

compass, but perhaps of most significance for the state's future was his survey of the overland route to Adelaide that only Edward John Eyre had travelled before him. Forrest trekked in a small party with Nyungar guides and dreamed that the same journey might one day be made by train. The idea of the Indian–Pacific train route was such a central demand of Forrest's at the meetings to decide upon Federation that had the other states not agreed to the plan Western Australia might well have remained independent.

Forrest was initially opposed to Federation and although he legislated for the right of women to vote, his motives were political. He hoped that by allowing the wives and daughters of the land-owning class to vote, the voice of the more radical and largely male population of the goldfields might be diluted. As a result, in 1899 Western Australia became only the fourth colony in the world where women had suffrage, behind New Zealand, South Australia and South Africa.

The colony had only recently become self-governing in 1890, and it was under Forrest, by now a stout, bearded and bull-necked man, that the state progressed from fully autocratic to partially democratic. Forrest belonged to the generation born of the first settlers, many of whom fulfilled their parents' best hopes regarding their accumulation of land, wealth and status, as well as their worst fears, specifically with regards to their often casual barbarism towards Aboriginal peoples on the northern frontier. Not only did Forrest claim to have shot several desert Indigenous people in self-defence, but his biographer, F.K. Crowley, said that Forrest's humble origins as the son of an indentured servant and his eventual success created in him 'social snobbery, laissez-faire capitalism, sentimental royalism, patriotic Anglicanism, benevolent imperialism and racial superiority'.

As premier, Forrest was fortunate enough to preside over the city's first gold boom, when the state's population swelled and Perth grew rapidly away from its river base. He was a great abettor of O'Connor's various projects, protecting him from interference and broadly encouraging the realisation of his ambitions. O'Connor is often regarded as a victim of his own success: his earlier projects had come in under budget and on time, making the problems associated with the Coolgardie pipeline appear worse. But the vacuum left by Forrest's departure for the national legislature, which resulted in four changes of state government within a single year, created the conditions that left O'Connor exposed to the criticism of parliamentarians and the ridicule of sections of the press. While there are apocryphal stories of O'Connor losing his temper and stamping on his hat, his daughters described him as a generous man who often fed strangers at his table and gave money to the numerous poor, and he was also a clearly sensitive man with an artist's absorption in his projects. But as an engineer, he was no naif, and he knew where he stood in the altered political climate.

At a recent lecture given in O'Connor's memory by his great-grandson Mike Lefroy and academic Martyn Webb, I was able to look at his original suicide letter. It's a tragic expression of pain and frustration, as might be expected, with an odd final flourish that indicates an engineer's enduring pragmatism. Having described how 'I feel my brain is suffering … I have lost control of my thoughts', O'Connor ends the letter with the tacked-on imperative, 'Put the wing walls on the Helena Weir at once!'

While it emerged subsequently that one of O'Connor's deputies was trading land on the projected route of the Coolgardie pipeline, by all indications it was the vicious attacks on O'Connor's reputation that most affected him. They were led by *The Sunday Times'* Frederick Vosper, a t'otherside firebrand who'd been imprisoned in Queensland for encouraging striking shearers to shoot their oppressors, and Irishman John Winthrop Hackett, a parliamentarian and newspaperman who went on to found the University of Western Australia as the first free university in the British Empire. Vosper described O'Connor as a 'shire engineer from New Zealand [who] has absolutely flourished on palm-grease ... Mr O'Connor is a palm-greased humbug', and this combined with the three official enquiries into the pipeline's progress is considered to have been the source of O'Connor's migraines, anxiety and insomnia, which eventually led to his suicide while of 'a rational mind'.

The reaction was immediate and heartfelt. Flags flew at half-mast across the city, and the following day all public offices were closed. Workers at the site of the Fremantle harbour project and Mundaring Weir were given leave to attend O'Connor's funeral, the largest in the state at that time. More than a thousand people waited outside O'Connor's home in East Fremantle, and many thousands more flocked to see the funeral cortege as it progressed slowly towards Fremantle Cemetery, with the acting premier and the chief justice as pall-bearers.

However, according to Martyn Webb, the University of Western Australia's Emeritus Professor in Geography, it wasn't the Coolgardie pipeline that was O'Connor's pride and joy — it was the Fremantle port, which he had 'in good spirits' showed visitors around the day before his suicide. There, a Pietro Porcelli statue stands in O'Connor's likeness, raised high on a narrow plinth, while bas-reliefs of the Mundaring Weir and Fremantle Port lie at his feet. Less than a minute's walk from my studio, Porcelli's representation of O'Connor faces towards the hills, although it once faced the opposite direction, seawards across the protective arms of the port walls. The commerce of the port has played out beneath this statue since its unveiling by John Forrest in 1911.

From where O'Connor's gaze now looks pensively downriver, his chin on his fist, dressed like a worker in overcoat and boots, he would have witnessed strikers dropping chunks of mortar from the Fremantle Traffic Bridge onto the premier's boat on Bloody Sunday, 4 May 1919; when striking dockworkers threatened to riot, then the gunshot and killing of striker Tom Edwards by police; and the reading of the riot act while the coffin of John Forrest, who'd died en route to England in 1918 to accept his knighthood, waited to be unloaded from a nearby steamer. He would have observed all of the comings and goings of the hundreds and thousands of migrants who arrived at the nearby Victoria Quay, some of them like Judah Waten's character in the short story 'Looking for a Husband', observing the Fremantle docks 'fiery even in the shade. Only the gulls splashing and flapping their wings in the water lay cool and unperturbed ... and everywhere harsh voices sounded.'

Many of the new migrants in the early twentieth century were met by A.O. Neville, the first head of the newly minted government department for 'Immigration, Tourism and General Information'. Neville, whose name is now associated primarily with the assimilation policies of the 1920s to the 1940s, was initially stationed in his little Information Bureau office by the port. From 1910 he and his colleagues boarded the *Lady Forrest* and greeted, in person, many of the 10 000 annual arrivals, presenting them with a letter of welcome and a card detailing the rates of pay for workers in country regions. This was part of a government-inspired and Neville-directed policy of spruiking the arid eastern wheatbelt as a place where largely unskilled urban Britons might, with the help of a booklet describing how to sow their first crop, make a go of hardscrabble farming. In one year, 91 000 brochures and postcards were distributed overseas, leading tens of thousands to pack up their belongings and emigrate. The stated aim was for the state to have a population of one million. This of course all took place during the time of the White Australia policy. Prior to 1901, many of the ships that entered the port bore Afghans and their camels. They camped out on the foreshore and in the nearby dunes, beside the woolsheds and the wheatsheds, fragrant piles of sandalwood heaped for export and the stacks of jarrah bound for Britain. Jarrah sleepers were used across Britain's extensive rail network, and many of the thoroughfares of London, Paris and Berlin were under-laid with jarrah and karri blocks, some to this day.

Perhaps in the quieter moments at night, when the stars are clear and the wind is blowing, O'Connor can see the ghosting of the past behind the living port and hear the chants of those elders whom Nyungar people believe sung O'Connor to his early death, as punishment for breaking the rock bar at the mouth of the river, and disturbing the Wagyl, or serpent spirit, who lives there. At low tide the bowed bridge of smooth limestone that looked like a serpent's back allowed Whadjuk men to cross the Derbarl Yerrigan, the Swan River, swimming the last short distance across to Manjaree, or what is now known as Bathers Beach on the southern bank at Walyalup, or Fremantle.

The limestone rock bar was also a great place to spear fish, because the narrow channel carried all of the marine life that entered and exited the river. O'Connor's port required the rock bar to be removed, which was done by drilling into the hard travertine limestone and laying charges. Dozens of men drilled down from shaky wooden platforms that extended across the river mouth. The rock bar acted as a partial weir before it was removed, but its destruction consolidated Perth's viability as a city. Until then, the natural deep-water harbour in Albany meant that mail and tourists were landed there, more than 400 kilometres southeast of Perth, and then transported to Perth overland. Most other shipping passed through Albany instead of Perth for the same reason. The blasting away of the rock bar opened the Swan River to the Indian Ocean, and therefore the city of Perth to the wider world, and in doing so changed the nature of the city forever.

The Plain

'The drive of much of our technology is to obliterate distinctions of place ... My hope is that Perth will become more parochial and that planning for it will become minutely topical: more so, and not less ... every small hill and valley, every limestone outcrop repays attention on a sand-plain.'

George Seddon, *Swan Song*

Standing on the crest of the Darling Scarp overlooking the Swan Coastal Plain, it's easy to get the impression that the height and mass and broad obstacle that the CBD represents is somehow more permanent than the encircling suburbs and their mostly single-storey homes nestled within trees. From this position, the suburbs appear much like camps on the margins of the city centre, tucked into bushland, spreading across the lowland plain as far as the eye can see. And yet this perspective is false, if only because it's the structures in the CBD that have been built and torn down, sometimes many times over, whereas the buildings that people choose to dwell in have mostly endured.

Many of the city's suburban buildings were constructed during the 1960s and 1970s, amid the great influx of British, Italian and Slav tradesmen whose skills translated into some of the best-made homes in Australia. They were often double-brick houses rather than brick veneer, with mostly Italian and Slav grano workers doing the limestone trenching, footings and foundations and English tradesmen the bricklaying, carpentry, plastering and painting. These houses were built to last, and the rapid suburban growth on the lowland plain and the influx of migrants also had the effect of elevating a lot of Australian builders and tradesmen into positions of authority: supervisors, foremen and small-business owners.

In the city centre, very few of the original nineteenth-century brick buildings remain, and you need to take a stroll down narrow Howard Street towards the river to feel what it must have been like. On the fringes of the city and across the suburbs, very little is left of the already minimal pre-1950s industrial landscape. Unlike many of the Victorian-era office buildings that were stuccoed to within an inch of their lives, the older industrial buildings rarely attempted to conceal the labour that went into their construction: every brick laid by hand, every tile, and the frame of every window. These rare buildings, such as the now retired Midland Railway Workshops, are some of my favourites. They have a texture; they catch the grime and show their age, but they also use cathedral-like windows and natural light to flood their great interiors.

Perth is a city where the bulk of the built environment has been constructed over the past fifty years. There's a general absence of this kind of texture and history, particularly among the city's newer buildings, with their tilt-up walls and traceless glass facades, and the feeling that they've been made by machines and assembled rather than built.

A large number of Perth's suburban buildings are less than fifty years old, too. That is time enough for the trees around them to grow tall, though, and Perth suburbs really only come into themselves once they are clothed in trees.

It's in the suburbs that a majority of life is

lived, albeit largely without performance, without witness and mostly without record. The suburbs are Perth's quiet places, but this silence can have many qualities. For some, who don't take it for granted, it can be a source of peacefulness, even of spiritual satisfaction. For others, it can generate frustration, the sense that life is passing them by, brought on by the feeling, as described by Shaun Tan, of being 'somewhere and nowhere at the same time'. And yet the suburbs are also where Perth's most vibrant enclaves can be found, places such as Leederville, Scarborough and Bassendean, Victoria Park and North Fremantle, Mount Lawley and Subiaco. The bars, pubs and restaurants of these areas attract both locals and visitors, but fewer of the suburban kids looking for kicks who descend upon the nightclub precincts of Fremantle and Northbridge at night.

It's hard to imagine a city where the suburban pace of life is so closely linked to the gentle oscillation of the seasons and therefore the truest personality of the plain. Even in the unloveliest of suburbs, the sky arches from horizon to horizon, the sun passes unhurriedly across the usually blue sky, the stars and moon are clear at night. And many Perth residents choose to holiday somewhere even more relaxed and silent, where there are even fewer people, or at least likeminded ones, places such as Rottnest Island, or the surf breaks up and down the coast, or the quiet campgrounds of the karri forests or the beaches of the Great Southern.

Outside of the CBD, any attempt to build higher than a few storeys is usually met with fierce resistance. The issue isn't the amount of land that the buildings require, but that they eat into the sky, making the city feel smaller, less open to the horizon. It's almost as though to be a resident of lowland Perth is to carry the openness of the plain within ourselves, and to yearn in its absence. When I read of the young Western Australian soldiers in Brenda Walker's novel *The Wing of Night*, trapped between the Mediterranean and the limestone ridges of the Peloponnesian scarp, it didn't seem at all unlikely that a newspaperman finds them 'longing for the coming fight', homesick, as they are, 'for the open country behind the Turkish trenches'.

It usually takes extremity to disturb the seemingly tranquil air that sits over the land: riotous parties and car chases, fights between suburban gangs, and meth labs going up in flames. Perth's suburbs are sprawled enough so that it's easy to ignore what happens over the horizon – out of sight and out of mind.

At a break during a recent public lecture at the Alexander Library in Northbridge, I overheard one well-heeled woman tell her friend how she'd gotten 'lost in Armadale' as she started out on a trip to the south-west. Genuinely disturbed, she muttered, 'It's like a different country out there! Lucky I had my GPS!' Her friend consoled her with a pat of her hand, but I didn't sneer as I once might have. Only a few years previously I'd spent an afternoon in Armadale trying to track down a friend who'd just been released from jail, to pass on a message. When I found him, he told me about the speed dealers in the house two doors up who kept him awake all night with their fighting, their kids out on the streets. Even worse, some of the other local kids had found out about his wife's terminal cancer and kept breaking in to steal her morphine. He felt more like a prisoner than ever, he told me, and I felt ashamed to recognise how alien the poverty that characterised his state-housing neighbourhood seemed, after two decades living mostly in Fremantle. It occurred to me, too, that over the previous years I'd been to Melbourne and

Sydney more often than Armadale, or Midland, or Kwinana, or plenty of other places in Perth that I usually only visit when my son plays football there or I'm interviewing people for a story.

In my own immediate neighbourhood it's the presence of so many children that breaks down the sense that each house is a fortress of privacy separated by fence, verge and street. Their noise, disorder and fence-hopping play is also a demand for community, and I'm often reminded of the migrant's courage of a friend of mine's parents, Phil and Wendy, who live in Gosnells, a suburb in the south-east of Perth. Along with nearby Kelmscott, it has retained its sense of being one of the earliest of Perth's riverside villages. My friend's family were 'ten pound Poms' who came out to Perth in the 1960s and initially lived in the migrant camp at Point Walter. They had decided to leave Nottingham, move to the world's most isolated city and never look back. They bought their first suburban Thornlie home at a time when their mortgage repayment was $10 a week out of Phil's potential bricklayer salary of $200 a week – far more than a teacher or nurse or bank clerk earned then. For this reason, Phil has always thought of Perth as a worker's paradise.

Now in their eighties, Phil and Wendy are still an indispensible part of the multicultural street's community, and they still open their home to the neighbourhood kids, who over the decades and generations have always turned to them for companionship and advice. Like everywhere else in Australia, Perth's suburbs are full of people like them, who came to make a home in a quiet street but also helped create a stable community, a place that few people are interested in, perhaps, but which for the past fifty years has been the centre of their world.

At a barbecue recently in Fremantle I chatted with a builder and 'eco-property' developer who was over from England to renovate his sister's new suburban home. In England, he's only able to receive council permission to build on the condition that every house is identical to every other house, down to the letterbox and doorknob. He found it surprising to learn that so many Perth residents over the years have been allowed to build a home of their own, free of council interference, one that reflects their budget and personal taste, even when others might find that taste questionable.

It's certainly true that architectural profusion appears to be the only constant in Perth's suburbs.

The price of Perth real estate may have everything to do with location, and easy access to the beaches and city, but while the streets in the richer suburbs may be leafier, the houses larger, the gardens better tended and the cars more expensive, by and large the only regularity is the irregularity of the streetscapes, the same parched parks and bore-stained walls, the same alternating 'Marseille' terracotta and corrugated iron roofing.

The most substantial difference between the newer suburbs and the old is due to the fact that when the older suburbs were conceived there wasn't the machinery to grade the individual blocks, or to infill each subdivision to make sure that it rose above the water table. As a result, what is appealing about the older suburbs isn't that they are leafier, and therefore cooler in summer, but that the blocks rise and fall upon the crests and swales of the hardened limestone dunes that roll inland across the plain. Each house and street conforms to its original and cambered landscape, and often some of the original flora remains. Newer suburbs are generally bulldozed and re-contoured with powerful machinery according to a design predicated upon the level, taking out all of the native bush in one sweep. The broader vista of unremitting flatness only emphasises the sameness of the housing stock, the stunted imported vegetation and the same predictable suburban retail franchises.

Both in its absence and abundance, water defines life in Perth today. The reliably generous winter rains that give Perth its Mediterranean climate, and its higher annual rainfall than either Melbourne or Hobart, have been in decline for decades. The low-pressure systems that spin like mop-heads off the roaring forties in winter are no longer making it as far north, leaving Perth's dams increasingly empty. Two desalination plants are operating but there is still more demand than capacity, placing greater strain on aquifers such as the Gnangara Mound that have always been called upon in times of need.

Perth was originally a watery place, defined by the ocean on one side and the river flowing widely through, regularly flooded due to the high water table and the wetlands that filled and ran over. These wetlands were not only a valuable food source for the Nyungar, supplying gilgie and turtle, birdlife and yam, but were also identified by Europeans as islands of fertility in the sandy expanse of the coastal plain. Western logic understandably identified the land that supported the tallest trees as the most fertile, but this was shown to be incorrect. In fact, the tuart, jarrah and marri woodlands flourish best in marginal soils, and market gardeners, often Chinese, who were unable to secure riverfront land in the 1890s began instead to cultivate the soils of the numerous lakes and swamps that form part of the broader Perth wetlands.

There has been a lot written about the coastline as it relates to Perth's sense of itself, as both a margin and space for reflection, but the absence of the wetlands in this picture suggests something else about their place in the city's consciousness. Once covering twenty-five per cent of the Perth area, the string of swamps that run north–south along the coastal plain are all that remains after eighty per cent of the wetlands have been reclaimed. Large areas of the CBD and Fremantle are built on reclaimed land. Central Perth was the site of a string of lakes, of which only a few remain, and Fremantle was built on a promontory topped by Arthur Head, behind which a brackish wetland ran in a string up its stony white spine. As a result, the water table sits very high. Freshwater springs still flow beneath Perth's streets, and in both the CBD and Fremantle many buildings are fitted with pumps to clear basements of water.

The suburbs of Perth expanded away from the rivers and train lines early in the twentieth century. Town clerk William E. Bold's plan to create a series of garden suburbs that would function as commuter dormitories took in first the old lime kiln area around what is now Floreat Park and City Beach, and many of the intermittent swamps were either filled or encircled. If Robert Drewe is correct that Perth residents of his generation regard the beach in a nostalgic light because so many had their first sexual experience there, then perhaps the memories associated with the numerous swamps are more significant to childhood, an age that could yet find wonder and mystery in what were often degraded and rubbish-strewn points in the developing suburbs.

Of no interest to vandals, too creepy a place for sexual liaisons, too sandy for joggers, too scribbly for picnickers, the swamps were perfect for children. The peaty smell of rot and decay, the tea-coloured water, and the reeds and banksia and

gnarled paperbarks that resemble exhausted old
men give the swamps an ethereal atmosphere, suit-
able for all kinds of fantasy. The presence of can-
nibalised car wrecks, old campfires and paperbark
lean-tos only reinforce the swamps as a place of
refuge, the kind of place parents never visited.

When my mother was a child, it was still the
case that even in the heart of suburban Perth,
vacant blocks remained mostly in their natural
state: quarter-acre islands where balga, wattle
and hakea stood upon a carpet of wildflowers
such as hardenbergia and boronia, kangaroo paw,
blue leschenaultia, orange cat's paw and often the
donkey orchid. This was so when I first moved to
Attadale, in Perth's southern suburbs, as a child. It
was a newly developing suburb that held numerous
patches of remnant bush blazing with colour and
harbouring blue-tongue lizards, mopoke owls and
feral cats that were all wisely chary of kids. Perhaps they remembered the children of my mother's
generation, who often lit bonfires in the vacant
blocks, some of which got out of hand.

In winter, the swamps often reclaimed the nearby
land as the water table rose and the wetlands glided
in silver sheets across parks and roads and into
yards and alleys. I remember being fascinated by

this as a child, despite being accustomed to the long dry Perth summers and the sudden winter downpours. We depended upon those winter storms to irrigate our gardens. To my ears they contained all the drama of the foundry, with rain hammering on the rooftop and sheet lightning illuminating gouts of silver coursing down lengths of chain into forty-four gallon drums – and yet I was always startled by the capacity of the land to swell and silently bring forth water from its hidden stores.

One story that describes the importance of the wetlands to children is Tim Winton's 'Aquifer'. It is set in the kind of new suburb I associate most with my childhood, all building sites and newly watered-in lawns, edging out into the poor banksia scrublands. The narrator is a boy just as I remember myself: solitary but never lonely, happiest in whatever remnant bush he can find (although I was lucky enough to have parents who allowed me to wander, unlike the narrator). On one level, 'Aquifer' is about the passage of memory through time, the laying down of memory like sediment that speaks of belonging to the city. In the suburban Perth streets, the citizens perform the public rituals of claiming the new neighbourhood: regular maintenance of the house and car, keeping up the garden and lawns. The narrator, now an adult, learns that a child's bones have been found at the site of the original swamp, recently dried up because of the falling water table. This brings back memories, but although he returns to the swamp, now a crime scene, he does not share them with the police. They are private memories, to do with him and the wetland, and the presence of the police and media is like the intrusion of adults into what was the child's domain. The bones belong to the English boy the narrator watched paddling around the swamp on an upturned car bonnet, only to capsize and disappear forever. The body wasn't found, and the narrator had never informed the community of what had happened. And yet the narrator was haunted by the fact that in his eventual decomposition, the English boy would become liquid, part of the aquifer on which the swamp drew and upon which the citizens of Perth increasingly relied for their drinking water. Like Joe Lynch in Kenneth Slessor's poem 'Five Bells', the English boy has become part of the physical and metaphysical landscape, moving through the aquifer as the water seeps and runs, is drawn and flushed and dripped and evaporated and returned to its source, its mythic origins still present in the

silent and secretive 'waste-land' that the new city
has long forgotten.

The wetlands of Perth have always felt to me like
a secretive landscape amid the dry unconsolidated
plain, but even in their dampness they have suffered the same fate as much of the bushland that
surrounds Perth – the regular burning that myste-
riously seems to accompany school holidays. The
Nyungar were expert at firing the land to promote
the growth of pasture attractive to kangaroos, so
that the first settlers described seas of grassland
flowing around deliberately preserved islands of
forest. Unfortunately, the repetitive burning of
much of the bush inside the Perth area has dam-
aged what used to be a feature associated with the
landscape in winter and spring: the coming of the
wildflowers. Wildflower season is still popular,
but generally Perth residents need to travel to the
national parks in the Darling Scarp or visit the
wildflower beds in Kings Park to witness what
is one of nature's finest spectacles – the bringing
forth of carpets of delicate flowers of the brightest
tints from the most barren of soils.

If English author D.H. Lawrence had witnessed this spring ignition of the forest floor, the
main character in his 1923 novel *Kangaroo*, Richard
Somers, may not have viewed the burnt bush near
Perth as something so metaphysically threatening,
'so phantom-like, so ghostly, with its tall pale trees
and many dead trees, like corpses partly charred
by bush fires, and then the foliage so dark, like
grey-green iron. And then it was deathly still ...
biding its time with a terrible ageless watchfulness,
waiting for a far-off end ...' Despite Lawrence's
feelings of awe amid the silence and stillness of
the wandoo forest, had he stayed for spring and
seen the wildflowers of Perth then he might have
attributed to the bush a sense of fertility and
humour, too: a large part of the joy of walking
through knee-high flowers is the improbable riot
of colour, a laughing reply to perceptions of the
Perth bush as drab, inhospitable and humourless.

When I think of Lawrence's character and his
'roused spirit of the bush', I am always reminded
of the 'wrongness' of everything in Perth described
by the newly arrived George Seddon. This aliena-
tion from his new home became something that
he sought to comprehend, and he embarked upon
studies in local botany, geography, history and

geology. He was known affectionately around Fremantle as 'Professor of Everything', an acknowledgment of his erudition as well as his contribution to an evolution in the way Perth residents have come to view their environment. Peteris Ciemitis's wonderful 2006 watercolour portrait of Seddon, *Making Sense of Place #4*, hangs in Canberra's National Portrait Gallery and was a finalist in the Archibald Prize. It captures Seddon's piercing intelligence and wise-owl stare. His aged face contains all the colours and textures of an aerial map of the Perth landscape: the dark riverine lines and weathered blushes of red and blue stained by a golden light.

Seddon, who was born in Victoria and later worked in Europe and North America, arrived in Perth from Canada in 1956. His first impressions of the local bush were unkind, although not uncommon. He called the jarrah 'a grotesque parody of a tree, gaunt, misshapen, usually with a few dead limbs, fire-blackened trunk and hardly enough leaves to shade a small ant'. This is not too unlike a description of the jarrah, marri and tuart woodland from 1844, when settler Eliza Brown said that the trees were 'not handsome. It is seldom we meet with a perfect tree, they nearly all show a great number of naked branches and the trunks are in most instances blackened in consequence of the native fires ...' But Seddon, a man who realised upon his arrival that he was not Australian but Victorian, liked the city of Perth and its people, and so he stayed. However, it was his discomfort at the oddness of the Perth landscape (or moonscape, as others have described it) that precipitated his detailed and eloquent 'experience of the environment', something related in his four main books about Perth: *Swan River Landscapes*, *Sense of Place*, *A City and its Setting* and *Swansong*. This transition from a common early experience of distance to one of attachment essentially involved a change of focus, 'a learning to see' that required a perceptual shift away from the grander scenery that Seddon was accustomed to in Victoria and Canada, towards a focus upon smaller details, the secret life of Perth that ultimately provided him with sufficient nutrition to feel at home, newly warmed to its sense of place, a term that he might well have coined.

This is a process that I've seen duplicated in others, especially my New Zealander wife Bella. Accustomed to the striking mountains and rolling green canvas of her homeland, she initially felt locked out by Perth's dry air, bright coastal light and the lack of obvious scenery on the plain. She too acclimatised herself by learning to garden in the limestone soils. Soon she was attracted to the tough charms of the banksia and balga tree – the former whose leaves are like serrated swords, and the latter with its prehistoric aura, hard-earned flowers on long fibrous stems – and the sudden miracle of the dun-coloured scrubland flowering in spring.

I can remember the first time I saw the cover of Peter Cowan's 1965 collection of short stories, *The Empty Street*. I was in a second-hand bookstore, skiving off from my job as a supermarket trolley boy. I had never heard of Peter Cowan and didn't realise he was from Perth, but there was something about the painting on the cover that both fascinated and repelled me. It reminded me of being a bare-legged boy in the white-hot streets of my hometown. When I came across the book ten years later, in the library attached to the Australian Embassy in Tokyo, where I often travelled on days off to get a fix of Australian literature, I recognised the cover immediately, and the feelings

I'd had about it as a teenager and the images it had provoked came flooding back.

I sat down in one of the library's comfy chairs and immediately began to read, but I found I had to keep pausing to stare back at the staring boy who is the subject of the Robert Dickerson painting on the cover. I later discovered that the painting isn't of a Perth street, but that Cowan had requested Dickerson illustrate his book and had specifically asked for that painting on the cover. In any case, the hot glare that seemed to radiate off the painting despite the dullness of a Tokyo winter's day reminded me of Perth at midday in summer: the heat, silence and oppressive stillness, everything conspiring against movement. The boy is alone in the empty street that is composed of geometrically conforming lines, and even the sky is cut out into a single blocky shape, although everything is pale and sand coloured. The faces of the houses that front the sandy street are windowless and doorless, and high white walls block all of the yards. There are no gardens or footpaths or curbs. The child's one black eye stares out angrily at the viewer and the other is covered by shielding fingers, almost as if the sunlight hurts him. Robert Drewe, in *The Drowner*, describes the effect of the sky on the human figure in the summer heat of Perth: 'The sky was not a neutral ceiling for the landscape. It was a force. It pressed low on the low hills, forcing them to make a horizon with the river.' The empty street also appears spacious but oppressively close, and the boy seems marooned, much like one of the characters in Cowan's short story collection, 'alien as if they had never taken root in their environment, denied by the white bare rock'.

The protagonist of *The Empty Street*'s eponymous short story is psychologically riven, by day a white-collar drone and by night a murderer of suburban women. The narrative charts the murderous effects upon an apparently sensitive male of the dull suburban life that he's submitted himself to, a realm of thwarted desire that only finds true expression towards the end of the story when the character, as in so many Perth narratives of the twentieth century, escapes to the beauty of the hills, where he helps tend a nursery garden before his arrest. Unlike many other Cowan stories, however, where his characters come together in fleeting moments of blunt honesty and sexual communion before the silence and space of the suburbs untether them, 'The Empty Street' is all about concealment and what the muted spaces of Perth's flatland suburbs can mean to those who are vulnerable.

While 'The Empty Street' isn't Cowan's best-known work, it's perhaps his most fully elaborated text that plays on the theme of a Perth suburban gothic, something also explored in some of The Triffids' lyrics and Shaun Tan's paintings. The idea of a surface beauty floating mirage-like upon an undercurrent of aggression, and weirdness, is epitomised in Dorothy Hewett's poem 'Sanctuary', from her 1975 collection *Rapunzel in Suburbia*:

> This nervous hollow city is built on sand,
> looped with wires, circled with shaven trees.
> The bleeding pigeons tumble outside the windows,
> the children wring their necks.

Much of *The Empty Street* is set at night, when odd things happen in the suburbs, surreal moments that seem disconnected from the diurnal life of the streets but appear ignited by the dreams of the sleepers around. The return of the repressed, per-haps, leaching outside the boundaries of the picket fences and hedges and clinker-brick walls onto the narrow ribbons of black road.

Once, when a friend and I were returning from a party on a Fremantle backstreet, a driverless white HT Kingswood rolled over the crest of the hill, building up speed until it passed us and then crashed into a gnarled old peppermint tree and was silent. There was nobody around and nobody was roused. Another time I walked the same street at night and came upon a row of wheelie bins that had been set on fire, the hissing orange flames forming contorted holograms in the breeze. Again, nobody was roused. This was the hour when my beloved EJ Holden had been stolen a few years previously, just minutes after I'd arrived home from a party. At the sound of the hotwired ignition I'd raced out into the street, only to see the tail-lights float off into the gloom. I found the EJ the next morning, trashed and charred in the coastal dunes near the South Fremantle Power Station, alongside dozens of other wrecks. Only the alternator had been stolen.

I'm also aware of a friend of my brother's, a country kid who got drunk one night and walked the suburban streets, shooting out the streetlights with a .22 rifle, forgetting that he was in the city. Fortunately for him, and by now innocently looking for some company, he'd wandered over to say hello to a man sitting quietly on his front porch. The man was an off-duty policeman who'd just finished the nightshift and tackled him to the ground, restraining but protecting him from the black-clad Tactical Response Group who soon arrived in numbers.

The early hours are also the time most people associate with the crimes of Eric Edgar Cooke, the last man hanged in Western Australia. Between 1959 and 1963, Cooke murdered eight people and wounded fourteen more. The tabloid version was that Cooke was a night-time prowler, a pervert and house-breaker turned monster. He certainly terrorised the western suburbs over the course of four years, and his crimes have taken on a mythic status. He is often described in the media as the man single-handedly responsible for stealing Perth's 'innocence', at a time when many left their houses unlocked and their car keys in the ignition. Yet, by all accounts, to know Cooke was to like him, unaware of his secret passion for inhabiting the darkness.

Cooke's crimes have been directly or indirectly represented by writers such as Tim Winton, Peter Cowan, Robert Drewe and Dave Warner, although it was Perth journalist Estelle Blackburn whose research into Cooke's crimes exonerated two men who'd served time for murders that

Cooke committed, and admitted to committing, and brought to light the extent of his random violence against women. Her 1998 book *Broken Lives* is heartbreaking reading. The title refers not only to the men Blackburn helped exonerate, and to Cooke's blameless wife and children, but also to the numerous women who survived Cooke's attacks and have lived quietly with their fear ever since. The strong sense begins to emerge that in a spread-out city where the streets are claimed by sometimes violent men, the stories of Cooke's female victims and their experiences of another side of Perth's quiet streets would never have come to light if Blackburn hadn't given them voice. The fact that Cooke's crimes began only a handful of years after the National Film Board produced its now sweetly nostalgic *Postcard from Perth*, a cheerful celluloid picture of a city at peace with itself, hints at the complex layering of the silence in Perth's suburban streets and the sense that amid the quiet respiration of the sleeping city there lurks a presence that watches and waits.

Debi Marshall's 2007 book *The Devil's Garden* analyses the 'Claremont Killings', which, according to Marshall, were the subject of the 'most expensive and longest running case in Australian history'.

The forensic descriptions that detail the murder of two young Perth women and the disappearance of a third in the mid-1990s are chilling, as is the fact that during this decade some twenty women were abducted or went missing, never to be seen again. In the year leading up to the death of Jane Rimmer in 1996, the first of the two murder victims, there were two abductions and violent sexual assaults in the Claremont area, one of which, according to local newspaper owner Bret Christian, was never properly investigated and was only recently linked to the Claremont murders, and only recently solved.

But there is one story that is most chilling of all, as described by Con Bayens, who headed up Operation Bounty in 2000. The police operation was designed to clear street-walkers and kerb-crawlers out of Northbridge and Highgate, and it documented roughly 200 men a night being serviced by 350 prostitutes in the area. At one point Bayens, on patrol, saw a car that resembled an unmarked police service Holden parked in a side street. Assuming that the car was part of a drug squad operation, he acted only when he saw a sex worker enter the Holden. The driver was tall and impressive, and carried himself with the authority of a policeman, except that he was a civilian, who'd done a taxi-driver training course. In the boot of the man's car, Bayens found a kit consisting of 'zip ties, a balaclava, gaffer tape and scissors'. Worst of all, 'the boot was fully lined with plastic, top and bottom'. But the man couldn't be charged with anything and was let go. And nor was he thought significant to the ongoing investigation of the Claremont Killings, then focused on another individual. Which means that he is probably still out there on Perth's streets, driving around the quiet suburbs once darkness falls.

Perth was always a 'spread' city, with early settlements hugging the riverine and oceanic shorelines, but it wasn't until after World War II that it really started to sprawl. Government rationing of petrol and building materials ended, car ownership rocketed far beyond the estimates set forth in the 1955 Stephenson-Hepburn Plan for the Metropolitan Region, and the near full-employment conditions that endured for decades meant that for the first time home ownership was possible for the majority. Many of the migrants and workers who had inhabited the inner-city suburbs of East,

North and West Perth headed for the newly subdivided lots to the immediate north of the city.

It was suggested as early as 1904 that the best way to encourage the 'wage earning class' out of the 'rookeries and all tumbledown, unhealthy and decaying dwellings' was to push suburbs out into the bush, linked to the city by way of tram and rail. Allotments in the earliest suburbs had provided land, but other infrastructure and especially roads had to be funded by raising taxes from the homeowners of the immediate area. Clearing and building was often done by the locals, and the jarrah-plank roads that spread out of the city were often sourced, milled and laid by local workers and paid for by public subscription.

Perth is something of an unusual city in that, initially at least, the directions in which the city has grown haven't involved the replacing of arable land with housing stock. The riverine floodplain and foreshore market-gardens of the kind described so lovingly by T.A.G. Hungerford were never built upon, and until the coming of heavy machinery nor were the wetlands that were sources of fruit and vegetables well into the twentieth century. The important vineyards, orchards and market gardens in the Swan Valley, which to this day remains the wine-growing area closest to any Australian capital city, and the orchards in the hills and the Spearwood sands farmland along the south-eastern foothills also remained largely untouched by suburbia, mainly because it was vital to early administrators that Perth reduce its reliance on imported food. Perth's geographical isolation meant that until quite recently fruit and vegetables could never be bought out of season. This taught people to be self-sufficient – even in the richest suburbs, most people grew small amounts of their own fruit and vegetables.

One important exception to this setting aside of arable land was the dairy country just to the north, in what is now Osborne Park. In 1903, the areas north of the city remained bushland. According to one account, '[l]ooking across Beaufort Street ... from the site of the Mount Lawley subway, there was not a house to be seen.' But Perth's population grew some 700 per cent in fifteen years, and housing stock needed to be found. Osborne Park was named after William Osborne, who was a butcher and abattoir owner. He owned much of the land alongside the newly constructed Wanneroo Road (made of jarrah planks nailed down onto jarrah sleepers, to avoid buggy, and later automobile, wheels catching in the sand), and he initially got into trouble with the Perth Road Board for complaining about the unsolicited logging of tuart and jarrah on his land. Once subdivided, the area became popular with market gardeners and dairy farms (there were sixteen dairies operating in 1913), although at four miles from the city centre it was thought too far for many seeking land. There are photographs that document the arrival of the road and the building of the enormous Osborne Park Hotel in 1903, an island of white walls and shining roof. They give a good indication of the early endeavours to suburbanise areas away from the river, showing men and women wading around in the ankle-deep sand.

The 'build it and they will come' approach was clearly successful, then as now. Posters from the period mirror the real-estate spin employed today, and because many of the company owners had positions on the Road Board, they were able to direct extensions of the plank road out to their subdivisions in North Beach ('Perth's favourite watering place!'), or to 'Park Estate' and the optimistically named 'North Perth Extended' and 'Subiaco North' estates in Scarborough ('owing to the superior surfing at Scarborough, those engaged in this exhilarating past-time have "discovered" this new beach'), to Sorrento Estate and many more. Some subdivisions were clearly better planned and resourced than others, and there's a marked difference in the character of these early designs that can still be felt today. The part-owner of the Mount Lawley development, R.T. Robinson, as a member of the Road Board and a King's Counsellor, was able to bring a tramline extension to his new garden suburb. He also brought gas lighting, which was ignited in the evenings and extinguished in the mornings by a man who got about on a bicycle carrying a long tapering pole, like a medieval jouster. The suburb of Doubleview, so named because of its high position and therefore double aspect over the ocean and the Darling Scarp inland, was once characterised by the presence of much of its native bush, unlike other subdivisions of the era.

Some of the earliest suburbs, those of Floreat Park and City Beach, were shaped by the vision of William Bold, the prominent town clerk influenced by the automobile-centric garden cities he'd encountered in the United States, with their wide and beautiful boulevards. It took some time for his vision to be translated, however. Early residents of the two suburbs, living on land that had been used previously for extracting lime, complained of being isolated and forgotten. According to historian Jenny Gregory, one resident as late as the 1950s suggested renaming Floreat Park 'Noanulla – no shop, no footpaths, no sewerage ... very little transport.'

Which is not to say that the architects and bureaucrats of Perth as 'City Beautiful' didn't care. As elsewhere, there is a well-documented history of the early twentieth-century humanist struggle to create a planned city whose design would improve the quality of life of its residents. Councillors, architects and planners such as Bold, Harold Boas, George Temple Poole and later Paul Ritter were influential and clearly cared a great deal about Perth's future. As often seems to be the case in Perth, though, their best-intentioned plans rarely made it to fruition, stymied along the way by internecine feuding between councils and government departments, and the naysaying of the 'pragmatic'. For example, there was a plan suggested in 1900 to submerge the train line that bisected the inner city, replacing the surface area with a pedestrian space allowing freedom of movement between central Perth and Northbridge. This plan was only recenly realised, some 116 years later. The fixed-rail public transport branch-lines mooted to link the developing suburbs to the city were largely never built and are only recently back on the political agenda.

After World War II, the state government was heavily involved in development, initially using mainly prefabricated housing materials. The northern suburb of Innaloo, which was originally known as Njookenbooroo, and populated with largely European migrants (one described it as a 'real never-never land, with only a few weather-board shacks dotted around'), was one of the first to be developed, after Joondanna and Glendalough. It was followed by a public housing estate in Scarborough, although the largest project involved the building of the city of Mirrabooka, home to Nollamara and Balga, where nearly 5000 public housing units were quickly developed.

With Perth's recent growth in population, access to public housing has become more difficult than ever, although it's hard to remember a time when it wasn't thus. As early as 1947, mention was made of the tough conditions in some state residences in Scarborough. Many of the one-bedroom flats built there housed recently returned servicemen and their families, some with as many as thirteen children. One man in the flats known as 'the Alley', designed to be temporary accommodation, was told that he had no prospect of being allotted a state house because he didn't have enough children – there were only five in his family.

As Richard Weller, who was until 2013 the Winthrop Professor of Landscape Architecture at the University of Western Australia, points out, it's an inexplicable fact that despite the wealth generated by the recent mining boom 'homelessness rates in Western Australia ... are significantly higher than in other states.' This has a lot to do with the sad statistic that, according to the Community Housing Coalition WA, the state has one of the highest *second* home ownership rates in the world, but because of negative gearing and capital gains nearly one in ten properties across the state lie empty, simply because many of these landlords don't need the income. Meanwhile, just like in the 1890s when tent cities sprang up all over the place, with an estimated 1500 new arrivals every week, more and more people are forced to live in caravans, tents and cars.

Perth is not a city commonly associated with high-density housing projects, although there are some enduring and well-loved precedents. Architects Harold Krantz and Robert Sheldon focused their apartment-building outside of the city centre to make the most of the cheaper land. They were responsible over a period of four decades in the mid-twentieth century for building more flats than anyone else in Perth, often some thousand a year, from high towers to three-storey walk-up swollen houses. Although many Krantz and Sheldon buildings have been torn down, others remain and are some of the most distinctive buildings in Perth. The duo was described as introducing a continental European aesthetic into the Perth building market, and a modernism whose minimum standards now seem generous.

Krantz and Sheldon took a cautious but innovative approach to building. Aiming to produce housing that workers could afford, they chose not to become a publicly listed developer and instead funded their projects by subscription, in some cases designed to attract the investment of Jewish émigrés looking for a home in Perth. In the words of Harold's son David, 'We turned the clock back and tried to use traditional methods and traditional materials in better ways.' According to Harold, this method of employing a European functionalism within what the University of Western Australia's School of Architecture, Landscape and Visual Arts dean Simon Anderson calls their 'monumentalisation of the vernacular' is why 'they do not get old fashioned as quickly as a lot of styles do'.

Harold Krantz started out working for his influential uncle Harold Boas in the 1920s before setting up his own practice. He worked with Margaret Pitt Morison and John Oldham before he was joined in 1939 by Robert Sheldon, a Viennese Jew who'd escaped from Austria after the *Anschluss*. Their practice was later to employ dozens of architects newly arrived from Europe, many of whom, such as Jeffrey Howlett and Iwan Iwanoff, went on to design some of Perth's most distinctive buildings. Harold and his wife Dorothy were also great supporters of the theatre in Perth. Krantz designed the Playhouse Theatre in Pier Street (demolished in 2012) near where he'd met Dorothy, an actor in many local productions.

The bulk of Krantz and Sheldon's buildings that remain are dotted around the edges of the inner city and throughout the older suburbs.

Their best-known building is probably the Mount Eliza at the edge of Kings Park, nicknamed 'The Thermos Flask' because of its circular structure and finned extrusions, but my favourites are the humble walk-up red-brick apartment blocks. To me, they are distinctively Perth, somewhat run-down but often clothed in the cool shadows of gum trees. There is something about the Art Deco lettering and the blend of stucco, cement, brick and grille-work that reminds me of hot childhood summers and the imagined peacefulness behind the curved white balconies that resemble that staple form of my childhood – the curved hand shielding against a fierce sun. I think I was drawn early to these comfortable-looking buildings because of the atmosphere of nostalgia that I sensed around them, capturing both the faded glamour of old Los Angeles and a lightness of touch that con-trasted with the brutalist lines of the 1970s struc-tures going up on St Georges Terrace.

I still get a kick out of picturing Elizabeth Jolley high up in Krantz and Sheldon's Windsor Towers in South Perth (as described in Brian Dib-ble's terrific biography, *Doing Life*), a twenty-one-storey slip-form concrete structure commissioned by Alan Bond in 1969. Jolley worked there as a cleaning lady but also used the time to pen her outsider novels, looking down over the city where her clients were at work.

If Harold Krantz's aim was to move beyond the traditional Australian dependence upon the terrace and the villa, and in doing so create a minimum population density and hopefully a more vibrant social landscape, the vastness of Perth's suburban sprawl has always worked against this. As early as 1899, Perth's inhabitants were reported to be 'dispersed over a wide area rather than their concentration within comparatively narrow limits'. Today, with a projected population increase of thirty per cent over the next decade, and an anticipated population of four million by 2050 (from the 1.8 million resident in Greater Perth), state governments are slowly rethinking the long-held bipartisan view that public transport infrastructure is a cost and car ownership an investment in economic growth. In Richard Weller's book *Boomtown 2050: Scenarios for a Rapidly Growing City*, some of the statistics are telling. Not only has economic growth in Perth rivalled that of China over past years, but combined with the city's anticipated growth, the most radical according to Weller that has been seen in an Australian city to date, it's also the case that '[a]pproximately 70% of Perth's new residential development still occurs at or beyond the boundaries of currently developed areas'.

This continued sprawl will not only continue eating into woodlands but will exacerbate Perth's dependence on the automobile, in a city that already has the fourth highest car ownership ratio to population in the world, in what is 'one of the most sprawled (120km long) cities on earth'. The idea that Perth is a paradise for many of its migrants has a long history, but due to climate change – Perth has had four of its hottest years on record in the past five years – the suspicion that it's a fool's paradise is something altogether more recent. Tim Flannery's comment that Perth might well become the twenty-first century's first ghost metropolis is well known, although it was made at a time before the desalination plants came online. It's clear that in the future Perth residents will become more dependent upon what Tim Winton calls our new habit of 'drinking the ocean'.

The post-war boom in Perth that led to a rapid doubling of population gave rise to the creation of the northern suburbs, but more recently much of the new suburban growth is taking place in the north-eastern and south-eastern corridors. For the first time in Perth's history, much of the new development is replacing arable land that has been used to grow food for the city. With the population set to double by 2050, Weller's point is that 'the entire infrastructure of the city will have to double. *Everything* that was built in 179 years will have to be built in forty.' In *Boomtown 2050* he makes a case for different types of development, pointing out that the 'business as usual' model will simply mean that 'Perth will become a 170km long city, a flatland of suburban sprawl covering more than 200,000 hectares of land.'

Each of the different scenarios Weller proposes involves the development of high-density housing, from suburban infill to apartment towers lining the arterial highways, the coastline, the scarp. All are a response to the central question: where will we fit another two and half million people over the next few decades? The NIMBY attitude that has developed in the city, much of it as a response to what was regarded as the desecration of Victorian-era Perth, coupled with a traditional lack of political enthusiasm for public transport and the ancient Perth prejudice towards 'flats', is unlikely to change in the near future, meaning that the business-as-usual model of suburban development is likely to continue, resulting in the intensified clearing of bushland that is both ancient and highly biodiverse.

As Weller points out, much of the costs of suburban sprawl are hidden. It's a remarkable irony that the aristocratic dreams sold to the earliest European settlers, where a family might own a house and a sizable acreage of land, has been realised in the suburbs of Perth, although the farmland and energy resources and labour required to maintain the suburban landowner's house and lifestyle are hidden from view. Weller estimates that to sustain an individual in Perth's current housing stock 'takes 14.5 hectares of land, seven times the world average. Western Australians, Saudi Arabians and Singaporeans share the increasingly dishonourable status of being the most unsustainable people on the planet.'

It's perhaps telling that K.A. Bedford's 2008 Aurealis Award-winning sci-fi novel *Time Machines Repaired While-U-Wait* describes a 2027 Perth little different from the current city, only amplified. The comic novel's protagonist, 'Spider' Webb, lives and works in Malaga, still a battlers' suburb. His workshop is one of a number of 'countless, ugly, concrete tilt-up structures built in Malaga over the past few decades', nearby one of a number of 'sprawling northern enclaves, all … monster homes and malls so big they had their own weather, permanent residents and airfields on their roofs …'

The City of Light

'Perth felt like a peripheral place not just
physically but in a lot of other conceptual ways.
Peripheral in a positive way, implying great
possibility and opportunity, a certain license to
muck about in the backyard, invent your own
meaning without great consequence. I often
wonder if I would have felt as liberated growing
up in a bigger city, surrounded by a more self-
consciously artistic culture or family – maybe not.'

Shaun Tan, *Suburban Odyssey*

I'm meeting a friend for a beer in The Print Hall,
one of the bars and restaurants that are part of the
transformation of Brookfield Place on St Georges
Terrace. Newspaper House and the WA Trustee
and Royal Insurance buildings remain clustered
at the foot of Brookfield Tower, the new branch
office of BHP Billiton and a skyscraper that

predictably reflects the monumentalism of a global mining giant.

The Western Australian economy has doubled in size over the past two decades, but unlike during the flashy 1980s, when the wealth was largely paper money and its projections onto the city seemed both lazy and insensible to issues of identity, of late there appears to be a more considered attention to design and an eye to permanence rather than a quick buck. The costs involved in the restoration of Newspaper House and its neighbouring buildings, now home to upscale bar and dining venues the Heritage and the Trustee, must have been considerable. These buildings were derelict for many years, and there's evidence of both a painstaking attention to detail and gold-rush extravagance at the Trustee, of a kind not seen perhaps since the days of John De Baun and Claude de Bernales. The custom-made solid pewter bar weighs in at an incredible twenty kilograms a linear metre.

Inside Newspaper House, the high ceiling of the atrium and the tabloid-shaped windows flood the hall with a crisp light. The print-room odours of molten lead, hot ink and heated paper have been replaced by the hoppy scent of boutique beer in elegant glasses, freshly shucked oysters and mullet toasties. It's the time of year when the heat and winds are receding, coming into my favourite season. The high-contrast summer light has softened, too, and everything has taken on a crystalline definition.

Ask many Perth expatriates what they miss about the city and the answer is often the light. It's not a romantic or a nostalgic light, not the playground light of our childhoods, but a light so clean and sharp that it feels like an instrument of grace, seeing a new world with new eyes. Because the days are cooler, and the sun warms rather than burns, the pleasure in the air means that it's almost impossible not to be happy. Days like this remind me of Nyungar man Barry McGuire's comment that the reason Perth is so relaxed, so 'wait a while' and seemingly at peace with itself, so quiet and still at night, is because the songs of this place are still being sung, the place is still being 'looked after', even if not many people know this.

It doesn't surprise me to hear that in the Nyungar language there are different words to describe the different qualities of the local light — the warming, glowing morning light (*biirnaa-ba*) that shone down on us the previous week, for example, seated on iron chairs at an outdoor restaurant overlooking the river. It also doesn't surprise me to learn that according to the Nyungar dreaming, light once encompassed everything; everything started with the light. Barry explains how, in a time when every bird, animal, rock and tree shone with its own internal radiance, the trickster moon convinced the kangaroo to reveal the name of its sacred illumination, and in doing so the kangaroo became separated from it. This fall from grace started a chain reaction. As the moon went about stealing the light of everything, darkness was introduced into the world, even as the moon became brighter. Now light only exists alongside darkness, although the daytime light is still the pure expression of that sacred illumination.

The Print Room bar is packed with an office crowd of lawyers, public servants and executive types. There's a strong whiff of money in the room, but it's still a Perth gathering: informal and a bit raucous, no neckties or power suits. We admire the refurbishment of the hall, designed to replicate the pages of a book, each room containing a differently themed restaurant and bar, but there's plenty of original detail left over from its previous incarnation as the home of *The West*

Australian. The conversation turns naturally to the newspaper, Australia's second longest running and now a monopoly daily, and some of the characters and personalities in some of the rival papers going back to the nineteenth century.

Most of the early Swan River colonists tended to restrict their writing to diaries, or memoir, absorbed as they were in trying to make sense of their new environment. There wasn't much written about Perth in the form of poetry or fiction until the twentieth century, and this was generally published in the local newspaper. As a result, the story of personal and political expression in Perth was played out most strongly in the often short-lived newspapers of the nineteenth and early twentieth century. In competing with *The West Australian*, and before that its ancestor, *The Perth Gazette*, these papers tended to attract extreme personalities. One of the first was the 'stormy petrel' William Nairne Clark, another young Scotsman who emigrated to the colony. After a duel fought in Fremantle in which he killed his opponent, the lawyer by trade saw an opportunity for a contrarian voice in the media. The mouthpiece of the government, *The Perth Gazette*, printed things like the following, in reference to a Nyungar who'd stolen a ram: 'A trial of this notorious offender would appear to us unnecessary, as it would incur expenses to the colony and much inconvenience to the prosecutors' (in other words, Goordap should be shot without trial). However, Clark's *Swan River Guardian* counter-punched with statements such as this: 'No sophistry can conceal the fact that Western Australia is a conquered Nation, but still another fact stares us in the face; that we ... must abide by the consequences of that first act of aggression which was sanctioned by the British Government.'

The idea that the Nyungar were somehow justified in evincing 'their repugnance by a thousand acts of hostility' was predictably not a popular one. Clark's various assaults on a government that brayed like a donkey 'from its rear' meant that the *Swan River Guardian*'s life was cut short. Clark eventually left the colony for Hobart.

Of the many newspapers that sprang up after the *Guardian*, some were sober journals and some were mouthpieces for their editors' opinions, focused on conducting bitter personal rivalries with other editors. These feisty rags must have provided an entertainment of sorts, because some of them lasted for a considerable time and gave rise to the careers of men such as John Curtin,

Frederick Vosper, Charles Harper and John Winthrop Hackett.

There was seemingly room enough for everyone in the newspaper business of the late nineteenth century, as long as you were male, had a thick hide and a keen sense of humour. My local newspaper, *The Fremantle Herald*, was started in 1867 by three ex-convicts and tailored to appeal to a largely working-class audience. The three editors used the forum to critique the convict system and challenge the ruling elites up in Perth, but like many papers of the time it also included local poetry and prose. This was before political hopeful John Horgan named and shamed what he called the 'six hungry families' of Perth, as part of his unsuccessful attempt to get elected to the state government's upper house, the Legislative Council. Horgan felt that these families and their kind ruled to further their own interests, while ignoring the plight of the more numerous. Horgan was sued for libel and fined the significant sum of £500. But Horgan ran for parliament again two years later and successfully defeated one member of the 'hungry six' by a handful of votes. He drove the eight-hour-a-day agenda but there was little he could do to undermine the sense of entitlement of the older families.

The Perth newspapers seemed to attract many from the first wave of migration from the eastern states who, like Horgan, brought with them a welcome dose of radicalism and fearlessness. The most notorious and fondly remembered is the distinctively tall and pale Cornishman Frederick Vosper, who was one of the best-known faces in Perth at the time. In the era of the ubiquitously bearded and moustachioed European male, Vosper's cleanly shaved jawline, long black hair, sharp nose and dark clothes made him stand out from his peers. Before coming to Western Australia, Vosper had been imprisoned in Queensland as one instigator of a strikers' riot. He had earlier suggested, in print, that Charters Towers shearers ought to let their oppressors 'feel cold lead and steel; as they have starved you, so do you shoot them'. As an inmate, his head had been shaved, and he'd vowed never to cut his hair again.

Vosper made a name for himself in the gold-mining regions of Cue and Coolgardie, with his trade-union politics and his ability to rouse a crowd and cut down hecklers and fools. His response to being asked 'What is alluvial, anyhow?' was to reply that the questioner should 'Go home, my man, and have a really good bath. After you have done so, let the water run off you, and have a look at the result. That is alluvial.'

When Vosper was elected as an independent to the state government's lower house, the Legislative Assembly, he moved to Perth, married a widow and drew on her money to start up *The Sunday Times*. Among other things, he used the paper as a mouthpiece to hound John Forrest for what he saw as ducking the issue of better representation for the miners of Coolgardie. Vosper had exploited the vehicle of an earlier newspaper to attack what he called Forrest's 'makeshift devices and supine, spineless ideas of statecraft', as well as the cosy relationship of rival paper *The West Australian* with Forrest's government. Unlike Horgan before him, however, Vosper achieved some significant wins in parliament, including the introduction of a minimum wage for state-contracted workers and a successful inquiry into the treatment of female inmates at Fremantle Asylum. He died aged thirty-one of acute appendicitis and is remembered both as a political reformer and the leader of the attacks that felled C.Y. O'Connor, as a man Vosper considered too close to Forrest.

By the early twentieth century, future prime minister John Curtin was another actively engaged in the sometimes brutal world of Perth journalism, as editor of the *Westralian Worker*. Victorian by birth, Curtin had gone to jail for his anti-conscription activities during World War I, and his mentor Frank Anstey had convinced him that the imagined quieter waters of Perth would be beneficial to Curtin's health and career. Like many successful adoptees of Perth, Curtin assimilated into the suburbs, living in a small cottage in Cottesloe from where he caught the train to work every day. Despite being defeated after one term in Fremantle by an independent candidate and local butcher, Bill Watson (evidence of Perth's enduring preference for strong local personalities rather than party-political candidates), Curtin was a great bridge-builder and organiser, and he did a lot to forge a stronger link between the industrial and political wings of the Labor Party in the 1920s. But in his early years as a doctrinaire socialist, penning editorials that included such phrases as 'the bowed back of labour can expect to have the stinging lash of unemployment applied unrelentingly', Curtin wasn't above the kind of petty (if sometimes amusing) name-calling that seems to characterise the period. One such spat occurred between Curtin and J.J. Simons, founder of the

Young Australia League (YAL), who together with Victor Courtney had started up *The Mirror* in 1922.

Ron Davidson's loving biography of the newspaper, *High Jinks at the Hot Pool: The Mirror Reflects the Life of a City*, describes how Simons and Courtney's paper filled a niche by supplying Perth citizens with up-to-date sporting results but also gossip and innuendo. Robert Drewe, in *The Shark Net*, describes witnessing his father lurking suspiciously by the incinerator in their suburban backyard, 'reading avidly' through *The Mirror* before consigning the 'sex and scandal sheet' to the flames. But it wasn't always so, at least not until the editors (one of whom was later Ron Davidson's father) figured out that sex and scandal in a buttoned-down and largely blue-collar city kept the readers coming back.

J.J. Simons was not only a part owner of the 'clean dirty' paper *The Mirror* but also a Labor parliamentarian with the nickname of 'Boss'. He was also adept at marrying his political message with his editorial agenda, one that was often about 'the villainy of his many personal enemies'. He engaged with Curtin over the matter of Simons' own resignation from the party, the result of what he considered to be the machinations of a 'secret junta.' Curtin felt that Simons was determined to make a martyr of himself, and he ran the front page of the *Worker* with a headline spread over three columns: THE LATEST AND GREATEST OF ALL THE MARTYRS! SOME REFLECTIONS CONCERNING A SWOLLEN HEAD ...' and an article that hinted at Simons' mercenary reasons for abandoning his post and splitting the Labor vote, ending with 'Too much prosperity is not always a good thing, as witness, that of the tapeworm – JC'. According to Ron Davidson, Simons hit back immediately by labelling Curtin 'the wobbly worker', a reference to his drinking problem, and 'the journalistic odour from the Yarra'.

Alfred Deakin had seen Simons' public speaking and had tipped him as a future prime minister. In a measure of the levels of political engagement at the time, Simons attracted crowds of 2000 people to his rallies in East Perth, within a total constituency of only 5000 voters, but it wasn't enough to get him elected. He withdrew to build Araluen, in memory of his beloved mother, now a popular park in the Perth hills, and to run the *YAL* and *The Mirror*, from where he could safely take pot-shots at his enemies.

Courtney and Simons' approach had been made clear in an earlier incarnation of the paper, *The Call*, which had baited the mayor of Perth at the time, William Lathlain, for his sycophancy towards the crown and favouring of conscription, among other things. They were sued for libel, although the jury only awarded the mayor a farthing in damages. The following week, according to Ron Davidson, the '*Call* featured its peace offering – a big picture of Lathlain wearing a mayoral chain of farthings'. It's a very funny picture, with the farthings prominent beneath the mayor's stern and unsuspecting stare, and must have driven Lathlain mad with frustration.

Part of *The Mirror*'s success was its use of humour to cock a snook at the pretensions of what then passed for high society in Perth, as well as to 'suppress the suppressionists': the killjoys and wowsers who pontificated about morality from the pulpits and lecterns and court benches but, if the editors of *The Mirror* are to believed, were also given to boozy orgies whenever the opportunity arose. *The Mirror*'s readers loved to hear about Bacchanalian goings-on in suburban Peppermint Grove among the 'naicest' families, 'the shameful doings of the Swagger set', or 'the Pseudo Western Aristocrats of Booze', as evidence of hypocrisy from on high.

The West Australian claimed to be a paper of record, whereas *The Mirror* stories 'came from the courts, with murders ... a specialty; from people oppressed by silly governments and bureaucratic bunglers; from germ ridden restaurants; and from the roving and quirky eyes of the paper's reporters'. While Davidson casts a clear eye on the early tendency of the paper to opine at the expense of non-whites, in particular the imagined sexual allure of the 'Celestials', the stories in *The Mirror* ranged from images such as 'STRANGE SIGHT NEAR CAUSEWAY ... A man, his wife and their small boy, armed with an axe apiece, were seen hacking into the carcass of a draught horse, stuck in the mud flats at the city's edge' to stories about lurking males in overcoats and female suburban streakers with 'CYCLING LADY GODIVA STREAKS THROUGH SUBIACO/ YOUNG MEN STARTLED AS SHE WHIPS OPEN HER COAT' (when truthful material was short). Detailed coverage of society murders became the paper's greatest attraction, so that after a taxi-driver's murder on Westana Road in suburban Dalkeith, this main thoroughfare was renamed Waratah Avenue to remove the stain brought upon the desirable new suburb by *The Mirror's* relentless coverage.

But the editors and journalists of the paper at least practised what they appeared to preach, that is, their celebration of the city's underdog characters. One of *The Mirror's* more successful pranks involved Percy Button, a well-known street acrobat and cadger about town, famously grubby and often charged with vagrancy for performing in front of the well-heeled crowd in queues outside His Majesty's Theatre in the CBD. *The Mirror* staff allowed Button to wash and often fed him in the alley beside their Murray Street offices. On one occasion in 1929, the staff journos cleaned him up, dressed him in a tuxedo, gave him a fine cigar and perched him on the stairs at His Majesty's Theatre, the site of many of his arrests. 'Do you know this man?' the paper's readers were asked, above a front-page photograph of the anonymous 'Perth silvertail', with a prize offered for the correct answer. Predictably, the paper's respondents identified him variously as the Prince of Wales, the Lieutenant Governor and the Duke of Cumberland, among others. 'Clothes maketh the man,' the paper wryly observed the following week when Percy's identity was revealed, which led in turn to *The Mirror* defending Button when he was next arrested for vagrancy and labelled by the presiding judge as a 'filthy disreputable sight'.

When Button was bashed by two policemen near Cottesloe Beach in 1931 for being a 'dirty looking cur' and then put before the mercy of the same judge, *The Mirror* was there to give Percy's side of the story. He wanted to earn his living his own way, as a 'handspring artist' and bottle collector, and besides, it was the Depression years and there was no work to be found. He was a returned soldier, who'd served with the AIF in 1917. The judge gave Percy one month's hard labour.

Another local character celebrated by *The Mirror* was Ernest 'Shiner' Ryan. He'd emigrated from Frog Hollow in Sydney, where, in 1914, he pulled off Australia's first armed robbery and getaway in a car. Shiner had spent a lot of his adult life in prison, and he added to his total in Fremantle. Ryan became a Fremantle legend, in a town 'crammed with characters'. Author Xavier Herbert, then working in a Fremantle pharmacy, described the port city as a place where:

> The narrow streets seemed always to be thronged
> ... The town itself was no less colourful than its

waterfront, peopled as it largely was by seafarers
and globetrotters that the ships of half a century
had left behind. The packed shops and restaurants,
the wine bars, pubs, hash-houses, whore-houses,
doss-houses, were run by people of all breeds ...
Of nights the bars fumed and roared, the drunks
bawled and brawled and wept and puiked, the
Salvos and their Brethren banged their drums...

Shiner Ryan was Fremantle's pre-eminent lock-
picker, able to pick a lock with his hands behind
his back so that he could stand innocently facing
the street while leaning back against the shopfront.
Unfortunately, because he was so expert, any time
there was a clean robbery of goods rather than a
'break-in', the police only had to check whether
Shiner was out of prison. While in jail he got into
trouble for forging coins that one of the warders
passed over the pubs of Fremantle, although he
became the first person to get the prison clock over
the entrance gates to run on time. The Fremantle
Prison museum still has two model white sailing
ships (which are quite shimmeringly beautiful)
that Shiner made of leftover porridge, ground
glass and salt crystals.

Ron Davidson's father, Frank, interviewed

Shiner often, on one occasion about a painting Shiner had done of Jesus, standing in the prison's no-man's land between cell-block and watch-tower, holding a lamb, except that 'it was a black lamb bearing Shiner's naughty schoolboy face'. The painting took Shiner back to Sydney, where a 'Sydney art authority' lauded it as a significant work. There he renewed his acquaintance with childhood sweetheart and Sydney identity Kate Leigh, who'd done five years for Shiner after per-juring herself to give him an alibi. *The Mirror* was there to welcome Kate when she arrived in Perth to take up Shiner's marriage proposal, 'an ageing woman ... in a giant straw hat, with fifteen dia-mond rings and a silver fox'. Midway through the celebrations, a teacher dropped in from the South Terrace Primary School with a request that Shiner pick a lock whose key had gone missing. The new-lyweds got into a taxi for the long drive over to Sydney, although the story goes that sixty-four-year-old Shiner only lasted 350 kilometres before he 'did a bunk through a public toilet, stole a car and returned to familiar Fremantle'. When Shiner Ryan died in 1957, aged seventy-one, Fremantle mayor Sir Frederick Samson was a pallbearer at his funeral. Kate Leigh, upon hearing the sad news, provided Shiner's epitaph, according to *The Mirror*: 'His brain was in his fingertips. He could open any lock with a coat hanger.'

Neither did *The Mirror* take the moral high ground when it came to describing the return to Perth of brothel-madam Josie de Bray, who'd been trapped in France and interrogated by the Gestapo during World War II. The brothels on Roe Street in central Perth, alongside the train tracks, had a long history. They were mainly small weatherboard cottages, except for Josie's, which was a 'custom-built villa with a piano in the vestibule' that Ron Davidson's Uncle Fred, a high-profile SP bookie, used to play when he felt the urge, since he wasn't allowed to play his grand piano at home. Wearing a Maurice Chevalier hat, he'd sing show tunes to the revellers and waiting customers. The brothels were built on Commonwealth rather than state land, with both the Perth Central Police station and *The Mirror* offices a mere couple of minutes' walk away.

During World War II, with the presence of thousands of American sailors, Roe Street was quarantined from the gaze of passing train passengers, after the Mothers Union successfully argued for hoardings to be put up to remove the view of scantily clad women sitting on the brothel verandas. Roe Street was such a part of 1930s Perth life that when Josie de Bray, the most famous of the madams, took a poulterer who'd set up shop beside 'Josie's Bungalow' to court for disturbing her custom (the sound of chickens being beheaded tended to cool the ardour of her clients), the judge ordered the poulterer to move and fined him £2.

Such was de Bray's authority that during her twelve-year absence, when her Roe Street brothel-keepers and accountant didn't know whether she was alive or dead, they reliably paid their rent and her commission each week. A terrific sum of money awaited de Bray upon her return. She had once warned a youthful Victor Courtney that 'You know, son, working on a newspaper is a dirty way to earn a living', but when *The Mirror* quoted her as saying that she intended to celebrate her return at the races, the paper was inundated with vitriolic letters because it dared to treat someone in the sex trade as a real person. *The Mirror* had crossed the line, and the 'fearful fifties' were upon Perth.

The one recurring theme from my conversations
with men and women from a Perth generation now
in their seventies and eighties, who grew up in the
city before the wave of new immigration in the
1960s, and before the advent of television, is the
celebration of the city's characters and the importance of local storytellers. I was lucky enough to
have a grandfather who was both a great racon-
teur and singer, and he could tell stories about the
people of Perth for hours, becoming earthier and
funnier as the night wore on. Perth may have been
geographically and to some extent culturally isolated, but there were the older traditions to maintain community memories of the characters who
peopled the city, as though their difference was
somehow the proudest expression of the city that
produced them.

I occasionally have lunch at The Buffalo Club
on High Street in Fremantle, one of the last places
in the city to serve pony glasses of beer. The club
manager, Leo Amaranti, himself in his eighties,
takes me upstairs to look at what is essentially a
shrine to one Perth eccentric, a man with the nickname of 'Matches'. Matches was a street person
who collected burnt matches off footpaths and
barroom floors to make his minor sculptural

creations. Eventually Leo, who is quite the character himself, put Matches to work with an unlimited supply of his favourite material. The result was two huge benches and high-back thrones made of matchsticks, shellacked a golden honey colour; the blocks of burnt sticks are arranged in parquetry formations that give the surfaces a three-dimensional effect. It's a wonderful piece of outsider art with an important function – the thrones and benches have always been used for official Buffalo Club meetings. Beside Matches' creation stands a heavy curved wooden bar liberated from the Aga Khan's luxury suite at a nearby hotel in 1987, following his visit to watch the America's Cup. The story of how the club members transported the bar from the suite across town and into the second-floor hall is an epic in itself.

In the window of the bar downstairs is a short narrative penned by Vince Lovegrove, who sang with Bon Scott in The Valentines during the 1960s. He and Scott were still teenagers, with Scott working as a postie and Lovegrove employed in a local menswear store. During their lunchbreaks, according to Lovegrove, they'd meet in the stands of the South Fremantle football club and 'plot and scheme about how we'd take over the planet and be the biggest band in the world ... but in the end, it was really about finding out where we fit in.' Lovegrove, who went on to a career in journalism, television production and managing bands, including AC/DC, Cold Chisel and Divinyls, was the person who later introduced Scott to Angus Young and Malcolm Young in Adelaide. The brothers were looking for a singer for their band, AC/DC, and Scott 'fitted in' so well that, of course, the rest is history.

Writers Niall Lucy and John Kinsella, in their recent collaboration, *The Ballad of Moondyne Joe*, take J.B. O'Reilly's 1879 novel *Moondyne* as a starting point from which to examine the meaning associated with the life of Joseph Bolitho Johns, by way of 'a work of the imagination informed by conversations on history, literature, philosophy and AC/DC'. Using a mixture of poetry, parody and reflection, the life of Moondyne Joe is drawn into broader discussions about colonisation, crime and punishment, and rebellion in Perth, demonstrating how Joseph Johns the historical figure can never be separated from the mythologised Moondyne Joe, the subject of song, photography, fiction and film (a feature film was made of *Moondyne* in 1913, although only the script that Lucy discovered survives). The authors discuss Moondyne Joe and Yagan, the Nyungar warrior, and Bon Scott, whose importance to recent Perth generations as a renegade figure approaches that of Moondyne Joe before him.

With the exception of Yagan, who was incarcerated at the Roundhouse Prison and then Carnac Island, what links O'Reilly and Moondyne Joe and Bon Scott is Fremantle Prison, something captured in the spirited cadences of AC/DC's song 'Jailbreak'. While Scott was only incarcerated there briefly as a minor before being transferred to a juvenile correctional facility to serve an eight-month sentence (for carnal knowledge of a minor and stealing petrol), the link between the other names – one that ensures their enduring cultural meaning in Perth – is the way that each thumbed his nose at the authorities, escaped custody and survived on the run.

One of my Fremantle locals is a pub called Moondyne Joe's. The dining room wall carries the 1874 photograph of Joseph Bolitho Johns that most people associate with his name. In it, he stands cheerfully dressed in workman's boots and trousers, wearing a well-used kangaroo cloak and carrying an adze. His hair is long and his eyes are friendly; his bearded face is set in a bemused smile. The fist that grasps the adze is strong and large, the hand of a workman. What's unusual is that the photographer, Alfred Chopin, took another photograph of Joe dressed in an immaculate suit, with a dandy's watch-chain, one hand stiffly on his hip and the other on the back of a bentwood chair. Joe's expression in this second, and largely unknown, photograph contains the same patrician rectitude of the many photographs of local Fremantle 'Merchant Princes' taken during the same period. That Perth has preferred the image of 'Wild Joe', the man who is alleged to have stripped off his clothes when in confinement, armed with an iron-age weapon, dressed in the kangaroo skin (the *buka*, or *boka*) of the Nyungar, suggests a preference in the culture for both the nostalgic perspective of a vanished frontier and the celebratory view of a very human hero, a very Perth hero, perhaps – much like Bon Scott nearly a century later. Littered with flowers and empty whisky bottles, Scott's gravesite at Fremantle Cemetery has become something of a shrine amid the loose grey sands that also contain the remains of Moondyne Joe.

One of my near neighbours in Fremantle, K, a man in his sixties, notices my four-year-old son's black AC/DC shirt and dutifully reminds me that the anniversary of Bon Scott's death is approaching. While Luka and K's grandson play with Jess, K's border collie, K says he makes sure to take his grandson to Bon's grave on the same day every year, and that he's not the only one. The numbers get bigger each year, he tells me, and plenty of them are grandparents taking their grandchildren along to show them Bon's grave and to 'show Bon his legacy'. K is a working man, not usually given to sentimentality. Perhaps overcome with the emotion of the looming anniversary, he shyly asks if he can show me something and proceeds to peel off his shirt to reveal a new tattoo of Bon on his upper arm. The lifelike Bon smiles the same mischievous smile he's often remembered by, one mirrored in the photographic portrait of Moondyne Joe, clutching an adze not a microphone, but with that same ironic glint in his eye.

In the six months before Fremantle Prison was closed in 1991, its medieval conditions highlighted by an earlier riot on a day when the temperature in the cells reached 47°C, the prison superintendent decided that art would no longer be regarded as merely a tool of control used to reward good behaviour. The traditional lock-down regime was relaxed and inmates were allowed to paint the walls of their cell and exercise yard as they pleased. The resulting artwork forms a permanent exhibition of the end of an occupation before withdrawal, telling of the different yearnings, the comic and tragic inscriptions of the incarcerated in the different divisions.

In the 3 Div exercise yard, which contained prisoners generally sentenced for violent crimes, there is a chilling but comically rendered floor-to-ceiling mural in lurid colours called 'Wayne and Willie's Swimming Lesson'. It depicts a river of blood, a rape scene, some mates drinking in a bar, a robbery in progress, a woman being dragged off by her hair. This image captures most people's worst fears regarding the minds of prisoners, the callous cycle of life of the recidivist criminal. But this painting is a minority in the broader gallery of paintings, sketches and scrawls. In the nearby cells there are the usual male and female genitalia painted around the teardrop-shaped judas holes in the heavy iron doors, needing only the guard's gaze to complete the satirical effect. There is the usual graffiti that like prisoner tattoos carries a coded language understood by initiates: spider webs suggesting entrapment; teardrops; Dali clocks with missing hands; burning candle stubs, especially in the cell of Bobbie Thornton, the state's first accredited tattooist, who ran a homemade tattoo machine with naked wires plugged directly into the mains power.

Over the wall from the 3 Div exercise yard is the identical exercise yard of 4 Div. It mostly housed lifers, many of whom had been on death row until 1984, when capital punishment was finally abolished. The artwork of the lifers is different from that of the short-term violent offenders. Gone is the cruel humour, replaced by a quietly reflective water mural painted by Peter Cameron, a Yamatji man, and Shane Finn and Erik Merrett. Although funding has lately been secured to protect the paintings from further damage, over the years the water mural has been slowly destroyed by damp. Its hauntingly beautiful portrait of water spirits from different Countries – the Wagyl, the Wandjina and Cameron's own characteristic water spirit – still covers the entire eastern wall of the yard. Cameron and Finn (who became a friend after I met him while teaching poetry at Casuarina Prison over three years) shared a slot on the highest floor of the division, and the walls and door are also covered with their vivid, charged and symbolically coded artwork. Beneath the whitewash in a cell across the row were discovered paintings done in the 1870s by convict James Walsh, now preserved behind Perspex screens. The paintings are classically influenced drafts of mainly biblical subjects and hint at the decorative work he did later in the prison chapel; they are quite different, though, from the paintings he created after his release, when he became one of the noted watercolourists in the colony.

In another nearby cell is a floor-to-ceiling painting by Kimberley man Reggie Moolarvie from the 1980s, an image of his home Country depicted in painstakingly stippled brushstrokes, a pointillist landscape clearly influenced by his time in Nyungar Country, with the characteristic 'Carrolup School' use of saturated pigments and melancholic/mystical hues. It fills the cell with a heartbreaking beauty and nostalgia, a fourth wall that works as a window onto another world. Despite the comings and goings of countless other inmates, black and white, the image was left unharmed for nearly a decade after Moolarvie's release; some thirty years later it remains in good condition.

But it is in another cell that the discourses of punishment and control, and artistic expression, are brought into clearest relief. On the ground floor of 3 Div, in a darkened space in a claustrophobically small slot, is a floor-to-window Nyungar landscape painted by Les Quartermaine in the Carrolup style. In the darkness of the slot the painting exudes a poignant light, an image of open forest that captures what Peter Cowan called the 'individuality, the strangeness and beauty' of the south-west landscape, the characteristic fluidity of the self-aware trees with their delicately rendered foliage, the darkness and depth in the foreground retreating beneath layers of soft light that carry so much feeling.

Quartermaine had been an inmate of Carrolup Native Mission in the Great Southern. One important difference between Carrolup and the Moore River mission came when Noel White arrived at Carrolup in 1945 to take up the position of headmaster. White encouraged his charges to go into the bush and paint what they saw. This wasn't without its difficulties, and White was often stymied by locals demanding the labour of the children, and officials who couldn't see the merit in teaching art to Nyungar kids. Either way, the initiative resulted in a body of work with a distinctive style characterised by a focus on landscape (at a time when Namatjira was a household name) and a richly textured palette of colours that captured something of the numinous qualities of a metaphysical Country. A selection of the 'Child Artists of the Australian Bush' toured Europe and ended up in collections worldwide, although the inmates were officially wards of the state and weren't allowed to receive any financial gain from their work.

The style has influenced many contemporary Nyungar artists, from Tjulliyungu Lance Chad to Christopher Pease, whose *Nyoongar Dreaming* depicts a human figure hemmed in by street-signs and poles and concrete barricades beneath an algae-coloured sky. Tjulliyungu Lance Chad, who has used the Carrolup style to depict the Swan River and the salt-eaten landscapes to be found in many places beyond Perth, also created a Carrolup-influenced landscape to form the cyclorama for the tragi-comic theatrical production *Binjareb Pinjarra* about the Pinjarra Massacre. In 1833, for an hour and a half, twenty-four armed soldiers and settlers fired continuously into a largely unarmed gathering of the Pinjarup clan, then hunted them through the bush, so that, according to J.S. Roe, 'very few wounded were suffered to escape.' The subject matter of the play is tragic, but it is leavened by what Nyungar playwright Richard Walley has called the wonderful 'humour born of the breadline, and a sense of the real worth of everyone no matter how down and out'.

The story goes that Les Quartermaine was stood over and forced to add another inmate's signature to his painting, although this might be apocryphal. The landscape is nostalgia in its purest form, but also a holding on to a source of strength. I have seen the painting many times now, but the last time I entered the cell I was taken by surprise – tears flooded my eyes. It was a gloomy winter's day and the cell was darker than usual, and yet the painting's radiant light completely overwhelmed me. Prisons are the darkest of places, and yet the images of light in the artwork left behind by Peter Cameron, Shane Finn, Reggie Moolarvie and Les Quartermaine, and the prison works of Walmatjari man Jimmy Pike, each carry the illumination of sharp observation and tender feeling amid a regime of exacting control.

When my father arrived in Perth in 1960 he found a city already beginning to grow away from its river base, but with remaining tribal loyalties to the older suburbs closer to the city. These loyalties were usually manifested in a strong identification with the different Aussie Rules teams in the state football league: Perth, West Perth, East Perth, Swan Districts, Subiaco, Claremont, East Fremantle and South Fremantle (subsequently joined by the Mandurah-based Peel Thunder in 1997). Perth seemed to him relatively multicultural. The city had a large Italian, Slav and Nyungar community, many of whom seemed to play footy.

My father at that time was a young flying officer stationed out at the Pearce Air Force Base. He didn't know anyone in Perth but had the perfect passport for entree into a sports-mad city: he'd played footy for the South Melbourne reserves in the Victorian league and for Launceston in the Tasmanian league; he'd recently won the Phelan Medal in the New South Wales league, despite being injured for half the season. Word had gotten around, and he was contacted by someone at West Perth. At the function to welcome him, there were speeches by the club president, Les Day, and the coach, former Footscray legend Arthur Olliver. Everyone made my father and the other new recruit, Collingwood star Ray Gabelich, very welcome, with invitations to dinner and drinks. Then it was straight into training, at what my father describes was a level and intensity he'd never seen before, even under Haydn Bunton, Jr. in the Tassie league. The first thing he noticed was that the sandy soil beneath the Perth ovals meant a fast track even on wet days and a game plan that suited speedsters. My father played in the centre as the replacement for Don Marinko, Jr. and speed was his big asset. And he needed it. His status as a new recruit and an officer with a double-barrelled name also marked him out for special attention – an assumption of privilege that was hugely at odds with his upbringing in rural north-east Tasmania. The second thing he learnt about the local conditions was that in the pre-season, when the temperature is often in the late thirties, it's a bad idea to scull a glass of icy beer straight after a game: cold beer into an over-heated body can cause instant paralysis. My father nearly died in the club change-rooms and had to be revived by the club doctor.

My father's league career was ended by an errant boot at the bottom of a pack, shattering his cheekbone and nose. He required reconstructive facial surgery, and 'Big Bear' Ray Gabelich and others from the club visited him often during his time in hospital, helping him through the long recovery — acts of kindness that my father's never forgotten. He also vividly remembers some of the great Indigenous champions of the day. He played alongside Bill Dempsey and against Ted Kilmurray, Polly Farmer and Syd Jackson from cross-town rivals East Perth. Later, Kilmurray, Farmer and Jackson would be the first of many Indigenous recruits to make the journey to the Victorian Football League, where their flair and speed helped shape the game that AFL football has become.

My father is not the first person to describe to me something that he found surprising about Perth in the 1960s, what he calls the 'wild-west admixture' of the time. Unlike other cities he'd seen in Australia, in Perth all the classes mixed freely and seemingly without rancour and, in football season at least, so did the 'races'. This was true at the local football games and still is. I take my son to watch South Fremantle play in the Western Australian Football League, especially the derby games against East Fremantle. The West Coast Eagles and the Fremantle Dockers may represent the state in the national competition, but in the WAFL games there is still a sense of local community and tradition. They are also far more relaxed and child-friendly than AFL games. In the breaks between quarters all the kids storm the field and play kick to kick, and punters wander over to huddle with the coaches and players and hear what is being said, or rather shouted. In the sometimes moody winter light and with the field crowded with hundreds of children and the soaring parabolas of hundreds of footys looping over and over, and the red-faced coaches shouting instructions within huddles of sometimes a hundred peering fans, the scene often resembles a Bruegel painting of a medieval public gathering.

Perth's obsession with sport has literally shaped the character of the city. Some eighty per cent of all open spaces within the city limits are sporting grounds, which are in turn used by only five per cent of the population on very rare occasions. The first mention of sport in Perth was made in 1829 by Captain Charles Fremantle, who'd been sent ahead of Stirling's settler ships to secure the high ground of Arthur Head, on the site of the town that would bear his name. Fremantle had fought on an American battlefield at the tender age of eleven, when he'd become for a period a child-prisoner of war. He was later the recipient of the first gold medal awarded by the Royal National Lifeboat Institution back in the old country, for swimming a rope through surf out into the English Channel to a wrecked Swedish ship. Having set up a rudimentary fortification on Arthur Head, Fremantle described in quite neutral terms the sport his men (presumably bored and pent-up after months at sea) were having slaughtering seals with tomahawks around Bathers Beach.

The first horse race in the colony took place a few years later, on October 2 1833, and further south, near where Tony Jones's C.Y. O'Connor statue sits out in the waves. A crowd gathered in the dunes to watch the race, eat ginger bread and be entertained by a 'lame fiddler' until the seven Timor ponies (one owned by Lionel Samson had the name 'More in Sorrow Than in Anger') set off down the beach – although the winner's name hasn't survived.

Whale watching also became a pastime for the residents of Fremantle, although not of the kind favoured today. Shore-based whaling in Gage

Roads was an important early industry to Perth's survival, and Arthur Head was a good place to watch the whaling boats paddle out to chase and possibly harpoon the passing Humpbacks.

But all this was before the introduction of football and cricket, the former especially taking hold and consolidating community identities. Bishop Salvado, who once kept his New Norcia mission afloat by giving piano recitals to the citizens of Perth, organised a Nyungar cricket team in the 1870s. This team travelled down to the city and not only regularly beat the locals but were enthusiastically cheered on by local crowds. In Bishop Salvado's journal, he describes:

> It is incredible how much excitement the New Norcia Cricket Eleven is causing. I have not stopped anywhere that they have not asked me about the New Norcia cricketers. If they were going to compete for a Chair in Theology or Canon Law, no-one would care about them, but if it is about cricket, what can be more important? They told me yesterday people will even come from York to see them play! Just imagine what a sensation it will cause if they manage to defeat the Perth and Fremantle cricketers!

And they did, on many occasions, although the team later disbanded when their white captain-coach Henry Lefroy gave it up to concentrate on running his station, which is a real pity considering the influence that Nyungar athletes have had on football.

My father's team, West Perth, was nicknamed 'The Garlic Munchers' because of its strong ethnic contingent, and the term wasn't derogatory. He said playing against the Fremantle teams reminded him of playing against Collingwood in the VFL, because the Fremantle crowds had a similar kind of feral intensity. The old Fremantle–Perth rivalry now enshrined in the Dockers–Eagles derbies started early, and so did the animosity. Ron Davidson describes one Fremantle–Perth game in 1892 that ended in a riot when the Fremantle crowd captured the umpire (a former Perth player) and beat him up, claiming bias. One of the Fremantle officials, Harry Marshall, by day an Essex Street baker and founder of the Lumpers' Union, shouted out, 'Bring 'em down and go for 'em. I'll pay the costs.' The umpire barely escaped with his life, and only then after the intercession of a Fremantle player. Marshall was charged and put in jail. When he'd done his time he was greeted at the prison gates by a marching band and large crowd, who cheered him through the streets. Soon after, and campaigning from prison on another charge, he ran for the state government's Legislative Council, and was elected – something that *The West Australian* newspaper called 'a disgrace to the whole colony'.

I can still remember traces of this atmosphere at the games I went to with my father in the late 1970s, particularly when Phil and Jimmy Krakouer were playing. Writer and academic Sean Gorman has used football in Perth to look at local matters of culture and identity, and in his book *Legends: The AFL Indigenous Team of the Century*, it's clear that respect was hard to come by given prevailing attitudes, although sport was one area this became possible. Ted Kilmurray changed the game with his invention of the 'over the shoulder snap' while running away from the goals, as did Polly Farmer with his use of the long handball. Then there was Syd Jackson, Bill Dempsey, Barry Cable, Stephen Michael and later the Krakouer brothers, who electrified the VFL when they first entered the competition (and are the subject of a terrific biography by Gorman, *Brotherboys*). And then there was that pivotal image in Australian sporting history:

in 1993, in what Gorman describes as 'both a delicately poignant moment and a statement of significant power ... either Nicky Winmar's most public private moment or his most private public moment', when Winmar, who started his career with South Fremantle, bared his breast to a taunting Collingwood crowd during an AFL match and defiantly pointed to his skin.

It's often said that a view of Perth is best appreciated from the heights of Mount Eliza, where you can look down into the city and observe the clouds playing across the mirrored surfaces of the glass towers massed by the foreshore. As George Seddon has pointed out, the 'oblique aerial view' of Perth from Kings Park, beneath the parapet of lemon-scented gums that leads to the War Memorial, has been recorded by artists and photographers from the first days of the colony. Whether it's the case that no other capital city in Australia has such a 'constant and universally preferred point of vantage', Perth's 'unparalleled visual record' is relevant mainly because it offers not only a picture of the growth of the city at the foot of the bluff but also a way of interpreting how perceptions of the metropolis have changed over the years, and how these most often represent 'aspiration rather than reality'.

The very first recorded image of a view from the site is a beautifully rendered painting by Frederick Garling, the official artist on Stirling's reconnoitre of 1827. The painting depicts an open woodland that is clearly the result of Nyungar firestick practices, near where kangaroo were driven off the bluff and into the spears of waiting hunters, and near where the recently constructed steel and glass walkway rises in a graceful arch through the tuart and marri forest canopy. What is curious about Garling's painting is that, unlike the majority of images that followed it, the view is concentrated upon the south, at the convergence of the Canning and Swan rivers, oriented towards the assumed new capital at Point Heathcote rather than the site to the east that Stirling actually chose. It was here that Stirling named the bluff Mount Eliza, after Governor Darling's wife, another offering to the benefactor who'd made the voyage possible.

Views of Perth recorded from Kings Park focus upon the low rise that St Georges Terrace straddles, sweeping round on the left and embracing the half-moon crescent of Mounts Bay, before the river disappears behind the city, with the Darling Scarp running in a corrugated line across the eastern horizon. The early sketches of Perth amid the tuart woodland spotted with settlers' tent and wattle and daub huts, small jetties and sailboats out in Perth Water, market gardens planted along the edge of Mounts Bay, each capture a tone of fragility and respite, the first tentative landmarks of western civilisation set against an illusory 'wilderness'.

Subsequent images depict the disappearance of the market gardens along the shoreline of Mounts Bay, soon replaced by an avenue of cape lilacs, through to the appearance of the town's first major buildings, although the tone is still Romantic, the image Arcadian. The elevation and the contemplative light allow the artist to frame the tranquil urban landscape from a hygienic distance, and thereby avoid the depiction of a village of expanses of hot sand between structures; the poverty of the majority of Perth's inhabitants; the soot and grime from the coal furnaces, cement works, brick factory and train station dusted across the facades of ageing buildings. On the shoreline, disease was rife for much of the nineteenth century, due primarily to the unsanitary conditions, although according to the beliefs of the time the culprit was the miasma, the presence of foul air emanating from Third Swamp (now Hyde Park) through to Lake Kingsford (where the train station is now situated), and from the shallow and increasingly polluted waters of Mounts Bay, all of which were reclaimed to varying degrees in an attempt to reduce flooding and rectify the problem of disease. In this context, the role of the south-westerly wind in blowing away the miasmic odours, believed to be responsible for diseases ranging from dysentery to ophthalmia, gave added importance to its traditional nickname: the Fremantle doctor.

Postcard pictures taken in the twentieth century do little to alter the Romantic perspective, although the delicate hand of the painter, so effective in capturing the almost supernatural clarity of Perth's early morning and late afternoon light, is replaced by the photographer's need for direct sunshine. Since the advent of colour photography in the 1940s, the pictures have maintained a remarkable consistency in their slightly over-exposed but cheerful tone. Photographs taken at night over the past decade hint at a new aspiration, suggesting a city of stimulation and nocturnal action: all neon, flashing beacons and fluorescent skyscrapers above a freeway streaked with traffic.

The images of Perth also reveal an evolution in the way that the Kings Park foreground is perceived, as well as a record of how it was transformed, according to the gardening fashions down the years. English country garden with rotundas and grottos and stone-bordered rose beds have given way to a contemporary preference for local native flora. Early nineteenth-century paintings of the park also contain idealised images of Nyungar, whose decorative function serves to reinforce the atmosphere of the pastoral idyll, while the trees are not recognisably Australian until much later. Kings Park is deservedly beloved by many, as a place where generations of children have played and adults have biked and walked, a place of celebration for families and wedding parties. The park is the site of the city's botanical gardens and the hugely popular wildflower festival; at four square kilometres it is one of the largest inner-city parks in the world, with two-thirds of the total acreage made up of native woodland interspersed with walking trails.

What is now known as Kings Park was set aside as public lands by Stirling and Roe in 1829,

although the park grew in size due to the intercession of Roe's replacement, the Surveyor General
Malcolm Fraser, and subsequently Premier John
Forrest, who, urged on by his forward-thinking
and botanically minded wife Margaret, expanded
the park's area in 1890 to roughly its current
1003 acres.

Margaret Forrest was a noted artist, and
although born in France to a French mother, as
the daughter of Edward Hamersley she was, like
her husband, among the first generation of settlers'
children. Margaret's painting career diminished
after her husband's election to the federal parliament in 1901, but she is remembered in particular
for being one of the originating members of the
short-lived but influential Wilgie Club (*wilgie*
is the Nyungar word for ochre), who practised
plein-air painting in the manner of the Heidelberg
School, and later as president of the Western Australian Society of Arts, but more particularly for
her wildflower paintings. Perth is situated in the
middle of one the world's thirty-four biodiversity
hotspots. With its distinctive flora, in particular
its numerous banksia varieties, there was a great
interest in botanical drawings to add to the collections of various museums.

As Jan Altmann and Julie Prott describe in *Out of the Sitting Room: Western Australian Women's Art 1829–1914*, after an invitation by Dr Mueller of the Melbourne Botanical Gardens, a few skilled Western Australian women were able to make a good living from botanical drawing, at a time when women were excluded from arts education in general. In particular, Margaret struck up two friendships with visiting British women, Marianne North and Marian Ellis Rowan, whose combination of detail and composition had greatly influenced the development of botanical illustration into an art form, primarily by locating the painting of flora within the broader landscape tradition. Margaret and Marian Ellis Rowan travelled extensively throughout Western Australia, but it's one particular painting by Marianne North (now kept at Kew Gardens) that illustrates the way these artists were able to redefine a genre by painting native flora *plein-air*, or on the site of its discovery. North's *Eucalyptus Macrocarpa*, painted in 1880, consists of the detailed depiction of the flower in various stages of undress, its sticky flowers containing hundreds of tiny floating arms like sea anemone. Because the flower is foregrounded against the backdrop of an inclined woodland, the eye slides off the image but always returns to the mysterious and vital flower that dominates the plane of view, and lends the painting a quite disorienting power. The story goes that upon hearing of the presence of a flowering Macrocarpa near Toodyay, the two women saddled their horses and rode eight hours to find and paint the tree.

The 'Fallen Soldier's Memorial' to commemorate those who died in the Boer War was built in Kings Park with a view over the city, on land sacred to the Nyungar. After the Great War came the 10th Light Horse Memorial and the Pietro Porcelli–designed Jewish War Memorial. The latter's foundation stone was laid by Sir John Monash and it is believed to be the first Jewish memorial in a public place in Australia. The defining feature of the memorialising landscape is the Cenotaph, an eighteen-metre Egyptian-styled obelisk designed by Sir Joseph Talbot Hobbs, who was a World War I general and divisional commander, as well as one of Perth's leading architects. Hobbs's Cenotaph was completed in 1929 and finally dedicated by Rabbi David Freedman. As Anzac Day grew in popularity the Concourse was constructed, and then, after World War II, came the Court of Contemplation, with its eternal flame set amid a pool of cool clear water, above the graven words 'Let Silent Contemplation Be Your Offering'.

If all this seems rather elaborate, this is because the Great War affected Perth, and indeed Western Australia, very badly. The state had only twenty-four years previously received its right to self-government from Britain, at a time when a majority of the population were London born, and many Perth residents still saw themselves as part of a 'land facing west'. Western Australia voted *for* conscription and fulfilled its expected quota of volunteers three times over. Consequently, fully one-quarter of the troops at Gallipoli were Western Australian. With more than 30 000 men and women volunteering, the percentage of volunteers per head of population was well above the national average; this enthusiasm is expressed in the tragic casualty rate of 53.7 per cent of those who enlisted, or some 18 000 men. That was nearly half of the eligible male population of Western Australia wiped out or physically and mentally debilitated, meaning that their families also became casualties of the war. One tragic example is Katharine Susannah

Perth

Prichard's husband, Victoria Cross winner Hugo Throssell. He took his own life after the war, after she had already lost her father to suicide.

My own father is a Vietnam veteran. Because of the hostility he and others encountered upon returning home, and the sensitivities involved, we were never brought up to particularly observe Anzac Day, although he began to march a few years ago in Tasmania. However, as a child in Kings Park it was hard not to be affected by one thing more than any other: the Avenues of Honour along the kilometres of roads that curl through the park, with each of the 1500 gum trees marked by an understated plaque at its feet that details the name of the dead soldier and the manner of his dying ('action' or 'wounds'). Most of the memorial trees were planted by family members, many in unison on 4 August 1919 at the anniversary of the outbreak of the war, when hundreds of the fathers and mothers and wives and children of the dead soldiers knelt in the grey sand down long sweeping stretches of limestone road.

In keeping with the tradition of utilitarian monuments, the park contains many seats and drinking fountains whose users are probably unaware of their original dedication. One the most popular statues within the park is the Margaret Priest–designed Pioneer Women's Memorial. This nine-foot bronze mother holding her baby is surrounded by stepping stones and bubbles and jets of water, designed to represent native trees of differing heights. The memorial is built near a Whadjuk women's place, a spring where the Wagyl is said to have risen to from the men's place at Gooninup, and a birthing site near a scarred tree. Much loved by children, who play in its cool mists, the Pioneer Women's Memorial stands in contrast to perhaps the oddest of Mount Eliza's memorials, perhaps because it is not actually in the park: the Edith Cowan Clock on the roundabout outside the park gates.

Edith Cowan was the first female member of parliament in Australia, one of the founders of the Western Australian National Council of Women in 1912, and a strong campaigner for the welfare of migrants and children. She lived near the park, but upon her death her supporters discovered that her memorial could not be admitted within its extensive borders.

The debate over the location of Cowan's memorial gives a representative picture of the struggle that she and others like her faced in the conservative

Perth of the 1930s. Whether it was because she'd offended someone on the Kings Park Board due to her activism or because the board was genuinely 'disinclined to favourably view the erection of further memorials other than national ones', the result was that the mayor could only endorse the placing of a monument to Cowan's memory at the gateway to the park, on council lands. Cowan's status as a defender of the underdog was invoked, her nurturing presence as homemaker, but it was the justification of a writer in a daily newspaper that is probably most representative of the discourse of the time, the fact that above all else '[s]he was an excellent speaker and a brilliant thinker. She was one of the best read women in Western Australia ... It has often been said that she possessed the mind of a man.' And so the six-metre Art Deco Donnybrook-stone clock that memorialises Cowan's service to the community, she who had succeeded in a 'male domain', the first public monument to an Australian woman, is actually a rather unremarkable clock tower.

I drive around Cowan's memorial on my way into the city, often negotiating tourist buses heading into Kings Park, although I'm never able to observe the memorial without calling to

mind the career of her contemporary, but sometimes rival, Bessie Rischbieth. Rischbieth grew
up in Adelaide, raised by her uncle and aunt. Her
uncle was a progressive politician and made sure
she received a good education. She married into
money, and after moving to Perth she became one
of the founding members of the Women's Service
Guild of Western Australia in 1909. Alongside
formidable working-class woman Jean Beadle, the
first-wave feminist Guild, under Rischbieth's leadership, went on to lobby for major reforms, which,
according to historian Kate White, included the
appointment of women police and justices of the
peace, the setting up of free kindergartens and
kindergarten teacher training, the improvement of
girls' educational opportunities, the establishment
of a monthly paper, and 'improved conditions for
women in government institutions, particularly
the Old Woman's Home and Fremantle gaol,
improved and extended nursing services in the
state; and, perhaps its most persistent demand, the
provision of a government maternity hospital'.

Rischbieth had a bitter falling-out with Edith
Cowan but pressed on both interstate and inter-
nationally. Having confronted Billy Hughes in his
Canberra offices after World War I, she persuaded

the prime minister to appoint an alternate female delegate to the newly constituted League of Nations, among other successful measures, so that, according to writer Dianne Davidson, 'In 1928 a visiting Victorian feminist hailed tiny, isolated Perth as "the Mecca of the Women's Movement in Australia" and the source of "streams of inspiration and knowledge to the rest of the continent."'

Rischbieth was trapped in Europe for the duration of World War II, but during her absence, the prime minister, John Curtin, finally instituted one of the Guild's main demands for a universal child endowment payment. After her return, she remained active in the women's movement, although she's mostly remembered for an iconic photograph taken in 1964. Only months before her death, aged eighty-nine, she stood by the Swan River in bare feet and raincoat and cheerful hat, holding a brolly above her head to protect herself from the rain, while blocking bulldozers at work reclaiming Mounts Bay for the Narrows Bridge project.

In a period that tended to create strong rather than pliable characters, both Cowan and Rischbieth have become intertwined in my memory with the type of unsentimental and forthright

Perth woman that I remember among the generation of my grandmother, who was herself a case in point. Despite strong ideas about how a woman should behave, and despite the limited opportunities available to women at that time, my mother and her three sisters have each remained creative and resilient and adventurous and, most obvious of all, comfortable in their own skins. Their Perth childhood was idyllic: they swam, surfed, danced, played in bands, painted, travelled and worked, part of a 1960s Perth generation insulated from the conflict and turmoil going on elsewhere in the world.

Something else that's evident from the view over the city at Kings Park is the length and breadth of the reclaimed land that now constitutes much of the city foreshore, although the scope of this expanse of grass is most apparent when on foot, crossing the foreshore in summer, the sun belting down and radiating off the hard-baked earth.

The Perth City Council's strategy has always been to adjust plot ratios for those developers prepared to facilitate pedestrian access and retail and dining options on the level of the street, but only recently has this been successful in terms of drawing people back into the 'dead heart' of the city. The revitalisation of many of the derelict buildings and alleys and arcades of the inner city, and the opening of small bars and restaurants throughout, has gone some way towards achieving this; however, one oddity often remarked about Perth is the continuing separation of the river from the city by the broad swath of grass that stretches from the freeway ramps beneath Mount Eliza to the Causeway Bridge at the other end of the foreshore, and still looks like the airstrip it once was.

If the Esplanade and Langley Park have become rarely used civic spaces over the past eighty years, this was not always the case. From 1885 until they finally closed in 1920, the Perth City Baths, with their beautiful Moorish cupolas at the end of a 300-metre jetty, were very popular. Following the closure of the baths, the equally popular White City at the foot of William Street, run by the Ugly Men's Association (who had a smaller, but similar site in Fremantle), was a fixture from 1917 until 1929. A kind of low-fi Luna Park, at a time when Perth city still hosted a residential population of workers and their families, White City was often described as a place for the common man and woman to recreate and relax. Run as a charity, whose funds went to Trades Hall, by day White City was a fairground with all of the usual side-show treats for children, including an open-air cinema and an enormous wooden slide, but also, according to Terri-Ann White – 'Boxing, Buck-jumping, Whippet racing and Games of Chance – Housey-housey and Sweat-wheels.' By night the dance floor came alive, and the brightly lit fair-ground became a place for the young to gather.

The fraternising between the young, the pos-sibilities for gambling and, even worse, commu-nication between whites and blacks, was what ultimately caused White City to be seen as the moral equivalent of the site's sewage problems, caused by the high water table and the often flooding river. Stephen Kinnane's book *Shadow Lines* refers to the importance of the place for ena-bling meetings in a space that allowed for relative anonymity. It might even be the place where his white grandfather and Miriwoong grandmother met for the first time, maintaining a love affair that survived long after A.O. Neville relinquished his power. It's for this reason, I suppose, that while White City is largely unremembered by the broader community, it seems to hold a special place in Indigenous memories of the time.

The new Elizabeth Quay project, despite the medieval thinking behind its naming (apparently when Premier Colin Barnett told Queen Elizabeth it was to be named in her honour, she responded that she was 'broadly in support of it'), aims to return the city to the lapping edges of Perth Water, and to bring back the pedestrians with it. I quite liked the original 'Dubai on the Swan' proposal put forward by the previous Labor government, with its towers and restaurants and large pool of circulating river water, although even the heavily compromised replacement design underway has been criticised for its potential to disrupt traffic – always a big no-no in car-centric Perth – and otherwise disturb the status quo.

As with every major development in Perth, the matter was bitterly divisive. Some mourn the loss of Perth city's 'front lawn', where Anzac Day parades take place and an enormous suburban barbecue was recently held for the Queen, and worry that the project creates a largely commercial zone out of a once public space. Some of those who support the Elizabeth Quay development are happy to see the interests of pedestrians put before traffic, for the first time in living memory – and it's certainly true that very few pedestrians in the city venture down to the river at Perth Water. During the state election of March 2013, won by incumbent Premier Barnett and the Liberal–National coalition, Labor leader Mark McGowan's gambit to win the votes of those disaffected by the Elizabeth Quay plans was a vow to compromise the already compromised project and halt the development altogether; he proposed a scaled-down group of structures beside the hurtling traffic of the freeway interchanges.

Perhaps it's true, as one senior architect I spoke to about the Elizabeth Quay project remarked, that a consistent development narrative such as 'Marvellous Melbourne', a response to and vision of the city in currency since the 1880s, with its implicit undertones of excellence and playfulness, might have made all the difference in Perth, too. Large parts of other cities were sacked in the name of building capacity, of course, but the scars in Perth seem to be deeper, the memories perhaps longer. The result has usually been willing compromise by tentative councils and politicians, and the kind of building characterised by the much derided but capacious Perth Convention and Exhibition Centre on the edge of the foreshore, which has variously been described as a thong, a thing, a barn, a shed, and is in no danger whatsoever of becoming an ornament to the city, in contrast to the new State Theatre Centre in Northbridge, with its finned facade and 1400 gilt bronze tubes hanging in a shimmering curtain inside, or the equally functional but visually playful Perth Arena. The Arena will stand next to the Perth City Link and King's Square development, which aims to join King Street in the CBD to Lake Street in Northbridge.

It remains to be seen whether the opportunities garnered by the most recent boom will be squandered as they were in the 1980s, or whether future mayors will be supported in guiding through promising projects to completion, developing in the meantime a culture of risk-taking with a focus on design quality, and in doing so create a more dynamic and populated city centre, as it was before all the people left and the corporations moved in.

It's lunchtime in Kings Square, Fremantle, and I'm sitting on a bench beneath the giant arms of a Moreton Bay fig, eating a Culley's cheese and salad roll in a poppyseed bun. The Culley family have been baking at their High Street tearooms for more than eighty years, and four generations later it's still a family business. I close my eyes and inhale the yeasty sweet smell of figs trodden underfoot that rises with the warmth off the brick-work, listening to the shouts of the drunks over by the library and the squeals of the children playing around Greg James's sculpture of Pietro Porcelli, another of my favourite statues in the city.

James has captured Perth's best-known twentieth century sculptor at work with a spatula, shaping a bust in clay; the everyman male head rests on a three-legged workbench at eye-level to its maker, bronze tools and off-cuts of clay laid beneath. The statue of Porcelli is so lifelike that newcomers often do a double-take walking past, and children are especially drawn to it, my own included, who love to reach into Porcelli's pockets and see what other children have hidden there: wrappers, coins, bottle tops.

Born in 1872 near Bari, Italy, Porcelli arrived in Australia aged eight, with his mariner father. He studied sculpture in Sydney and Naples, before travelling to Perth during the gold-rush with his father, along with the hundreds of thousands of others trying to escape the economic depression gripping the eastern states. Pietro's father gave up his life on the sea and instead set himself up in Fremantle on Pakenham Street as an importer of Italian goods. Porcelli junior's first sculpture was a bust of the premier, John Forrest, although the 1902 life-sized bronze of John's brother, Alexander Forrest, is better known. Shaped of Guildford clay before it was cast, the statue of Alexander Forrest stands on the corner of Barrack Street and St Georges Terrace, with Forrest dressed in his explorer's kit, rather than his mayoral garb. Porcelli also carved the beautiful brownstone Celtic Cross that stands in Fremantle beneath the 'Proclamation Tree', planted to mark the occasion of the colony being granted responsible government in 1890. He was also commissioned to do war memorials, and my favourite is the figure of Peace trampling on a sword, before the Midland Railway Workshops, memorialising the many rail workers killed in the Great War. Porcelli's most famous work, however, is his statue of C.Y. O'Connor on the Fremantle Quay. There is a poignant photograph of him standing beneath the clay model of O'Connor, dwarfed by the figure he's hand-sculpted. Porcelli looks frail, exhausted and slightly awed as he stares up at the model that when cast would be praised by John Forrest as 'thinking in bronze'.

Fremantle locals, particularly children, used to drop into Porcelli's studio to watch him at work sculpting, carving or doing a pour – something that Porcelli apparently never seemed to mind. When I visited Greg James earlier today at his J-Shed studio at the foot of South Mole, a minute's walk from my own studio, he too didn't seem to mind visitors. It's a crisp autumn day, and the air smells of saltbush and the pickled fish aroma of the aquaculture ponds across the street. As a friend of mine joked, only in Perth could a couple of overnight downpours result in the wettest March in forty years (before the hottest April on record), but the cool change and the dampness and tints of green in the heat-weary trees are welcome and refreshing. Down the beach the sculptures forming part of this year's *sculpture@bathers* exhibition are positioned along the sand and through the whalers tunnel and along the limestone tracks at the foot of Arthur Head, a sister exhibition to the annual *sculptures-by-the-sea* at Cottesloe Beach. There's something playfully appropriate about the scrap-metal statues of two horses gambolling on the beach; further along there's the lone woman beside the boardwalk, resembling a wistful bow spirit staring out to sea.

James was working on his latest commission, with the wide doors to his studio open to let in the light and sea breeze, and I asked him to describe a story I'd heard from Ron Davidson. James was working on the Porcelli statue in the 1990s, grinding it off in his Henry Street studio, when he sensed someone enter his room. It was late at night but James was used to visitors entering his studio around the clock. He turned off the angle-grinder so there was no danger of sparks catching in the visitor's clothes, only to look up and see Porcelli, wearing a blue cotton smock and baggy woollen pants, standing before him. The apparition walked through the nearby workbench on which sat bronze sections of his own torso and disappeared. It wasn't an unpleasant experience, according to James, but, a little spooked, he still invited his neighbour in an adjoining studio to join him for a cup of tea. What James didn't discover until later was that his studio had once been Porcelli's, a hundred years earlier.

A story like this in any other part of the city might seem a stretch, but Fremantle's old buildings are notorious for similarly phantasmic experiences, especially among artists who are usually the only ones working late at night. When my brother and I visited my aunt Patricia Hines at her silk-screening studio in the Fremantle Arts Centre in the 1970s, in the building that used to house the inmates of the Women's Asylum (and a place long reputed to be haunted), we were terrified by the skull of a *Batavia* shipwreck victim that used to be housed in a ground-floor diorama, and by the empty corridors after dark.

I finish my roll and bin the wrapper, climb onto my bicycle and pedal across the square, casting a glance at another favourite statue of mine: the 2002 Andrew Kay bronze of Hughie Edwards, slightly larger than life and dressed in his airman's uniform, staring up at the sky. He won the Victoria Cross and eventually became the most highly decorated Australian serviceman in World War II, but when he returned to Perth and became governor, according to Ron Davidson, none of Hughie's achievements or wartime excitements had matched the thrill of playing six games for his local team, South Fremantle, which were, he said, 'the most significant moments of his life'.

Cycling home to South Fremantle I pass Portuguese street artist Vhils inside a cherry-picker, working on the giant portrait of Fremantle-born Dorothy Tangney that's going up on the wall of the Norfolk Hotel. Tangney was Australia's first female senator in the federal parliament, a position she held for the ALP from 1943 to 1968. Vhils has characteristically worked in texture to the portrait by chipping away the layers of built history down to its gritty bedrock of redbrick and lime, in the process revealing a startling bas-relief image beneath the original layering of paint, stucco and cement. Tangney's face catches the afternoon light and shadows her eyes, making it appear as though she's watching the artist's bent back as he kneels and works the chisel.

It's getting on for late afternoon, and the light has softened across the sheoak woodland that rises along Blackwall Reach. Just out of our vision, kids are doing bombies from the thirty-foot drop into the blue river, but we've decided to take our own children to a northern riverbank to picnic at our favourite park. Around the corner from Chidley Point, the small wedge of grass on the edge of a newly retained shoreline is private enough to be relatively unknown, one of the reasons we like it so much. A few men in the car park are donning wetsuits and scuba gear, in preparation for a night-diving excursion to catch prawns with scoop nets in the deepest part of the river, and Luka watches amazed as the frogmen finish suiting up and begin to test their gear.

Down the stairs by the waterline, we share the foreshore with a Nyungar family playing cricket, while Max casts a lure off the end of the jetty, soon hooking and releasing a small tailor. Luka and his sister, Fairlie, wander the riverbank looking for jellyfish in the sepia shallows, but run to the jetty when Max spots a single dolphin, swimming back and forwards through the mussel-encrusted boat moorings. A black swan paddles over to sit quietly beneath the jetty, but is soon disturbed when the giant motorboats begin to return from their day-trip to Rottnest Island. In the rush to get back to their moorings in the exclusive yacht clubs upstream, the private launches speed past the Point Walter sand-spit, disturbing the smaller boats out crabbing in the bay, lashing at the moorings of the graceful old riverboats nearer to shore and grinding over the channel where the dolphin has retreated, finally smashing the otherwise peaceful shore with thigh-deep waves. It's the equivalent of being allowed to drive a tank down a suburban street, and a reminder that while the beach remains an egalitarian space, the river is less so. As the dusk begins to settle, dozens of the indistinguishable white giants round the point, one after another, their crew and passengers hidden behind tinted glass. The black swan washes around in the swell, its feet cycling to avoid being tipped.

Finally the river traffic dies down, and the sun sets over the bluff behind us. In the shadows, my children climb the elderly peppermint trees, counting how long they can hang from the rough branches before dropping. We are all alone now, except for the odd kayaker sweeping home over the still dark waters. The coloured lights of the city come on, and so do the channel markers deeper in the bay. The murmuring of crabbers hauling up nets. Hoots of laughter from across Point Walter, where a fireworks barge is being set up.

Festival season is nearly over, but there are still a dozen things we could be doing tonight. Perth's summer arts festival may be Australia's oldest, but it gets better every year. Tonight, friends are catching bands at an all-day concert, some of the 90 000 people who'll see music in Perth over the weekend. We're keeping our powder dry for the Nick Cave concert midweek and don't feel like we're missing out.

Bella returns with the kids' fish and chips, and while they pile in I wander over to the shoreline to sip my pale ale. I look at the quiet river and the dark ribbon of forest that runs along the limestone cliff; I smell the briny estuary settling on the evening air, 'perfectly warm, perfectly still'. My children laugh and squabble and scrunch the butcher's paper, and I'm brought back to them, the centre of my life these past years.

Perth is the city that I hope will nourish them, challenge and surprise them, growing — as they grow — into a city of commotion, spontaneity and opportunity. But there is more, too, if they want it. As I stand on the riverbank — lapping water at my feet, the smeary lights of the scuba divers edging out into the black depths, the smell of algae and salt and the dry bones of an old jarrah jetty, stars above me — I feel a sense of privilege, for things changing and things remaining the same, for knowing something of this place, feeling this place, and for the quiet gravitational pull of this force called belonging.

Postscript

When thinking about how to frame this postscript I was guided by something that one of my favourite writers about Perth, the polymath George Seddon, described when he wrote: 'a city may be haunted by parts of its past, and sustained by others.' This was another way of returning to that favourite quote of mine from Aboriginal writer Stephen Kinnane, included at the beginning of this book, where he describes 'the people of other eras that exist alongside our own, quietly watching the new psyche of the city take form ...'

It has always seemed to me that to be a writer, or anyone interested in the stories and the history of a place, is to live with ghosts – some haunting, others sustaining. A large part of the project I undertook when writing *Perth* was to give some limited honour to some of the ghosts that accompany me across any traverse of the city – Fanny Balbuk, Pietro Porcelli, CY O'Connor, Yagan, Bon

Scott, Edith Cowan, Moondyne Joe, my grandparents, to name but a few. Not all of the ghosts are human, however. The more I have learned about my city the more the spectral presences describing the plenitude of the original flora and fauna abide with me. Whenever I head into the city to meet a friend for a beer at Alfred's Pizzeria, for example, or across the road at one of the bars or restaurants inside the redeveloped Treasury Buildings, it doesn't take much to see beyond the walls and reimagine what James Stirling's botanist, Charles Fraser, once described in 1827 as the:

> ... quantity of black swans, pelicans, ducks,
> and aquatic birds seen on the river [is] truly
> astonishing. Without any exaggeration, I have
> seen a number of black swans which could not be
> estimated at less than five hundred rise at once,
> exhibiting a spectacle which, if the size and colour
> of the bird be taken into account, and the noise
> and rustling occasioned by the flapping of their
> wings previous to their rising, is quite unique in
> its kind.

Depending upon my mood, when I sit there on Barrack Street, I'm not only aware that I'm sitting beside the track of Fanny Balbuk, but I'm also drawn to revisit Fraser's enthusiastic descriptions of the incredible height of the ancient jarrah and marri trees rising over the ridgeline that contoured the Perth area; the number and character of the groves of casuarina trees; and especially the size of the *Banksia grandis*, which he described as 'often exceeding 40ft in height'. Another aspect of Fraser's avid description of the area, and something that was to become a feature of so many settler narratives, was his enthusiasm for the colour and variation of the region's wildflowers. Fraser admired the 'brilliant sky-blue' flowers of the blue pin-cushion, or native cornflower, the yellow and crimson flowers of the broom and what he described as a pink-flowered species of thistle, as well as the different species of flowering melaleuca, hakea, dryandra, wattle and grevillea. On the river flats, he wrote of great thickets of scarlet flowers and how the shores were 'covered with rushes of great height and thickness, concealing many beautiful plants, and a species of hibiscus'. One early settler, Emma Purkis, arriving in Perth during wildflower season, described how the town site's 'high hill running right down to the river and the bank ... was very beautiful in colours of green, yellow, white and pink, with small streams running at intervals into the river ... Where Government House ballroom now stands was a ravine and a running stream'.

Perhaps more than any other image taken of Perth, one photograph by Fred Flood, captured in the 1930s, of an ordinary semi-rural road in Jolimont, returns to my mind with an insistence and regularity that probably isn't normal. The photograph takes in the enormous size of an ancient 'King Jarrah' tree, dwarfing the horse and cart alongside. The tree, sadly, is no longer there, cut down for unknown reasons, as were all the others of its kind, especially those that were such a feature of central Perth and elsewhere across the plain. The last 'King Jarrah' that I was aware of, was cut down, suspiciously, by Main Roads on the planned route of the contested Perth Freight Link, because of an alleged complaint about a bees' nest, high up in its branches – the tree was thought to be five hundred years old. It was a tragic and needless end to a tree alive many centuries before the coming of Europeans to this shore, but it did, however, galvanise many thousands in the local community to stand in solidarity with a large parcel of remnant wetland long considered to be of vital environmental significance. As a local crime writer who has made a career writing into the gaps of the historical record in a city where, because of its relative isolation from other capitals, enforced silences have built up around certain key topics – the decision by the Barnett Liberal government to clear land for the construction of a private toll road (the Perth Freight Link), to a privatised port, should not have come as a surprise – but it did. Despite the discrediting of the project by noted scientists, town planners, traditional owners, anthropologists and various academics, and despite the daily presence of hundreds and sometimes thousands of opponents, many of whom were arrested by the dozens of police guarding a single bulldozer, the clearing went ahead in preparation for the highway to be built by key corporate donors to the Liberal Party. In the context of the absurd situation where the banksia woodland that once covered so much of the Perth coastal plain is itself now an endangered ecosystem, due to approvals for piecemeal clearing, alongside the fact that currently less than ten per cent of original Perth's wetlands remain, the project saw all of the usual ugly political truths about development in Perth come to the fore – politicians blatantly lying about the benefits of the project; manipulated decisions from within key government departments embedded with corporate interests, cheered on by the usual boosters inside West Australia's monopoly newspaper – the Kerry Stokes owned *The West Australian*. The 2017 election result did not go as planned for the Perth Freight Link project, however, and the incoming Labor government scrapped it as promised, having secured one of the most significant victories in Western Australian history. Good to their word, the ongoing restoration of the cleared site where I regularly walk with my children is encouraging. However, and despite their strong parliamentary majority, the state Labor government has also recently had to walk-back on plans to withhold a proportion of the heavily exported crayfish harvest for the local tourism market, due to industry pressure. Similarly, the EPA's recent plan to force natural gas companies such as Woodside and Chevron to offset their significant carbon emissions lasted barely a week before it was scrapped; again due to powerful lobbying efforts and lucrative advertising space taken out in *The West Australian*. *Plus ça change.*

Just prior to the original publication of *Perth*, we had an artist friend visit from Los Angeles. He had a photographic installation set up as part of the

Big Day Out, and was travelling the country with the bands and DJs. We took him on the usual tour, and later settled on our porch for a quiet drink. As someone who lived in an LA neighbourhood where one in eight people were homeless because of the GFC, and as someone who regularly travelled throughout the US, Asia and Europe, he described Perth as perhaps the last place on earth he'd seen where capitalism was still working. The state's most enduring mining boom was then still in full swing, of course, before the new reality dawned of boarded up shops and for sale signs everywhere, but it was a sobering thought in a city whose prime economic levers were geared toward the boom-time features of rapid population growth and its corollary – continual urban expansion and development – to the benefit of so many Perth developers over the years. A boom economy focussed upon export and primary industries means however that the inevitable bust is always around the corner, and it followed not long after our friend left, as indicated by the usual indices – falls in tax revenue leading to massive government debt, a rise in unemployment and severe mortgage stress in parts of the city. Perth has had its booms and busts before, of course, and while this will be of no comfort to those citizens who have lost their jobs and homes, most recently due to the COVID-19 pandemic, it remains a paradoxical aspect of the city that many of Perth's most treasured features are the result of fallow economic periods. Fremantle's Victorian-era streets, for example, are the beneficiary of a specific kind of economic neglect (and the latter efforts of heritage campaigners), namely an earlier unwillingness to invest in bowling them over to build newer buildings, as largely happened in central Perth. Perth's hills were never heavily settled due to a lack of economic opportunity. The Swan Valley was deliberately retained as an agricultural sector due to Perth's isolation from other markets, and now offers award-winning wineries and boutique arts and dining experiences while being accessible by river. Rottnest Island has always prided itself on its proletarian ethos, necessary due to Perth's earlier relative poverty, where all guests stay in tents or in government bungalows. The earlier impulses of men like Alan Bond to build Gold Coast–style towers along the city beaches was largely restrained by both local resistance and mitigating economic forces post the WA Inc period. Similarly, the recent practice of broad-acre land clearing on Perth's margins to build new suburbs has slowed during the latest economic downturn, allowing time to refocus the city's development narrative toward suburban infill and less ecologically damaging, higher-density living. The loss of short-term mining jobs in what is ultimately one of the most rapidly automating industries has also seen a growing commitment toward diversifying the economy by striving to improve tourism offerings, among other things, and the results appear to be paying off.

For my own family, and I suspect for most long-term residents of Perth, little has changed in the city over the past decade. In the CBD, the faithful redevelopment of the Cathedral Square site honours both aspects of Seddon's haunting and sustaining histories, including the construction of some of architect Kerry Hill's finest buildings alongside the immaculately restored State Buildings, using the original, locally sourced materials. Like most parents, as our children grow into young adults, we worry about the effects of climate change on their collective futures, reinforcing what my own post-depression era parents taught us as children of Perth – to conserve water, to respect and cultivate the plants native to this soil, to grow your own food, and to consume as little as possible. In the meantime, we follow the rituals – the beach in summer, camping in the desert in winter. Like the tens of thousands of others, my children and I take our seats at the new Perth Stadium, cheering our footy team having walked across the beautiful Matagarup Bridge. Whenever possible, we walk the dog in the nearby parks of remnant bush and wetlands among the native flora so wonderful to the early settlers, and so significant to the Whadjuk people's way of life.

A Nyungar friend of mine once described to me why Perth feels like it does – in particular its air of contemplative silence and expansiveness – its atmosphere of deep time, enduring. He said that Perth feels like it does, not *because* of the city built here, but rather in spite of it. To the attentive, he said, the Perth area still feels like it has *always* felt, just as it did before the coming of Europeans to this shore. This made immediate sense to me, just as it does in the forests of the South-West, or in the hinterland deserts – the sense of the quiddity of things foregrounded against an ancient landscape – the recognition that Perth, for all its best efforts, still feels strangely ephemeral, sitting lightly on the land.

Which is another way of stating the old

observation that Perth is a city where the land never sleeps, something for which many of its residents are grateful.

Acknowledgments

This book was made possible because of the advice, stories and materials shared by the following people: Shane Abdullah, Jeff Atkinson, Ron Bradfield, James Calligaro, Rob Campbell, Brett D'Arcy, Jo Darbyshire, Ron and Dianne Davidson, Brian Dibble, Ron Elliott, John Fielder, Paul Genoni, Maureen Gibbons, Liz Hayden, Ken Hayward, Dennis Haskell, Greg James, Wendy Jenkins, Geoffrey, Joan and Joseph London, Barry McGuire, John Mateer, Ken Miller, Carmelo Miragliotta, Jeannie Morrison, Mark Reid, Georgia Richter, Marty Saxon, Kim Scott, Ted Snell, Jon Stratton, Kerry Trayler and Glenn Hyndes, Brenda Walker, Antionne Yarran.

I'd also like to acknowledge the generosity of the following people for reading an early draft: Mark Constable, Ron Davidson, Sean Gorman, David Hutchinson and Deborah Robertson. Their suggestions towards a second draft were invaluable.

Ron Davidson and Barry McGuire were especially generous with their time, meeting with me on a number of occasions.

I'd also like to thank the librarians at the City of Perth Library, in particular Claire Burton, and the librarians at the Fremantle Library local history collection. As I researched this book, I began to recognise how important local publishers Fremantle Press (formerly Fremantle Arts Centre Press) and UWA Publishing (formerly University of Western Australia Press) have been in communicating and curating local culture over the years. It's hard to overstate how poor Western Australia would be without their books. Kudos to funding bodies, publishers and editors, past and present.

For readers interested in pursuing a more comprehensive recent history of Perth than I've been able to provide here, I wholly recommend Jenny Gregory's *City of Light: A History of Perth Since the 1950s*. I also recommend the various municipal histories of Perth that are too numerous to mention but are often crammed with fascinating detail (they are always available at your local city library). Ron Davidson's *Fremantle Impressions* is a brilliant rendering of the port city, its characters and stories, while his *High Jinks at the Hot Pool* provides a fascinating look at Perth through the history of a newspaper. If you are interested in reading more about the natural history and environment of Perth, I recommend each of George Seddon's books about Perth as well as *Ernest Hodgkin's Swanland: Estuaries and Coastal Lagoons of South-western Australia* by Anne Brearley. The fourteen books that form the 1979 Western Australian Sesquicentenary Celebrations Series are also great resources.

I would like to acknowledge the following people for their kind permission to publish quotes or for their help to obtain it: Georgia Richter of Fremantle Press, Terri-ann White of UWA Publishing, Robert Drewe, Nicholas Hasluck (all the way from Bolivia), Jenny Gregory, Gail Jones, Stephen Kinnane, Trisha Kotai-Ewers, Niall Lucy, Jan McCahon Marshall, Alsy MacDonald, Mark Reid, Brenda Walker, Dave Warner, Tim Winton, Jo Alach, Abby Page at Mushroom Records, Karen Throssell.

I'd also like to thank Joromi Mondlane of Mamba Boxing for the use of his boxing gym at all hours, and the noodle gurus at Cafe 55, iPho and Vivisen Teahouse for their sustaining broth.

Thanks to Phillipa McGuinness for inviting me to write this book and to Uthpala Gunethilake for carrying it through. I couldn't have hoped for a more thoughtful editor than Natalie Book. Thanks always to my agent, Mary Cunnane.

Thanks to my parents, Rosemary and Tony, for making those 3000-kilometre round-trip long weekends to Perth with a carload of kids (and the rest), and my brother and sister, Peter and Kerri, for their stories and advice. Finally, I'd like to offer my love and gratitude to Belinda and to my children: Max, Fairlie and Luka.

Bibliography

Adams, Simon, *The Unforgiving Rope: Murder and Hanging on Australia's Western Frontier*, UWA Publishing, Crawley, 2009.

Alexander, Alan & France, Victor, *Northline*, Fremantle Arts Centre Press, Fremantle, 1987.

Altmann, Jan & Prott, Julie, *Out of the Sitting Room: Western Australian Women's Art 1829–1914*, Press for Success, Fremantle, 1999.

Anderson, Simon & Nordeck, Meghan (eds), *Krantz & Sheldon: Architectural Projects*, Cullity Gallery, University of Western Australia, Crawley, 1996.

Bedford, K.A., *Time Machines Repaired While-U-Wait*, Fremantle Press, Fremantle, 2009.

Blackburn, Estelle, *Broken Lives*, Hardie Grant, South Yarra, 2001.

Bolton, Geoffrey, *Land of Vision and Mirage: Western Australia Since 1826*, University of Western Australia Press, Crawley, 2008.

Brearley, Anne, *Ernest Hodgkin's Swanland: Estuaries and Coastal Lagoons of South-western Australia*, University of Western Australia Press, Crawley, 2005.

Bridge, P.J. (ed.), *Daisy Bates, My Natives and I: Incorporating the Passing of the Aborigines: A Lifetime Spent Among the Natives of Australia*, Hesperian Press, Carlisle, 2004.

Bulbeck, Chilla, 'Breaking the Monumental Mould: How the Edith Cowan Clock was Built', in *International Review of Women and Leadership*, July 1996, pp. 86–90.

Butcher, Bleddyn, *Save What You Can: The Day of the Triffids*, Treadwater Press, Marrickville, 2011.

Carter, Bevan, *Nyungah Land: Records of Invasion and Theft of Aboriginal Land on the Swan River 1829-1850*, Swan River Nyungah Community Black History Series, Guildford, 2005.

Coughran, Chris & Lucy, Niall (eds.), *Vagabond Holes: David McComb & The Triffids*, Fremantle Press, Fremantle, 2009.

Cowan, Peter, *The Empty Street*, Angus & Robertson, Sydney, 1965.

Curtin, Amanda, *Inherited*, UWA Publishing, Crawley, 2011.

Davidson, Dianne, *Women on the Warpath: Feminists of the First Wave*, University of Western Australia Press, Crawley, 1997.

Davidson, Ron, *Fremantle Impressions*, Fremantle Arts Centre Press, Fremantle, 2007.

—— *High Jinks at the Hot Pool: The Mirror Reflects the Life of a City*, Fremantle Arts Centre Press, Fremantle, 1994.

De Vries, Susanna, *Females on the Fatal Shore: Australia's Brave Pioneers*, Pirgos Press, Brisbane, 2009.

Dibble, Brian, *Doing Life: A Biography of Elizabeth Jolley*, University of Western Australia Press, Crawley, 2008.

Drewe, Robert, *Fortune*, Picador, Sydney, 1987.

—— *The Drowner*, Pan Macmillan, Sydney, 1996.

—— *The Shark Net*, Penguin, Camberwell, 2000.

Drewe, Robert & Kinsella, John, *Sand*, Fremantle Press, Fremantle, 2010.

Easton, Leonard A., *Stirling City*, University of Western Australia Press, Crawley, 1971.

Elliot, Ian, *Moondyne Joe: The Man and the Myth*, University of Western Australia Press, Crawley, 1978.

Erickson, Dorothy, *A Joy Forever: The Story of Kings Park & Botanic Garden*, Botanic Gardens & Parks Authority, Western Australia, 2009.

Fennell, Philip and King, Marie (eds.), *Voyage of the Hougoumont and Life at Fremantle: The Story of an Irish Rebel*, Xlibris Corporation, New York, 2000.

Freeland, J. M., *Architecture in Australia: A History*, F.W. Cheshire, Melbourne, 1968.

Bibliography

Gibson, Ross, *South of the West: Postcolonialism and the Narrative Construction of Australia*, Indiana University Press, Bloomington and Indiana, 1992.

Gorman, Sean, *Legends: The AFL Indigenous Team of the Century*, Aboriginal Studies Press, Canberra, 2011.

Green, Neville, *Broken Spears: Aboriginals and Europeans in the Southwest of Australia*, Focus Education Services, Cottesloe, 1984.

Gregory, Jenny, *City of Light: A History of Perth Since the 1950s*, City of Perth, Perth, 2003.

Hall, Rodney, *Home: A Journey Through Australia*, Minerva, Port Melbourne, 1990.

Hasluck, Nicholas, *Anchor and Other Poems*, Fremantle Arts Centre Press, Fremantle, 1976.

Herbert, Xavier, *Disturbing Element*, Angus & Robertson, London, 1963.

Hewett, Dorothy, *Rapunzel in Suburbia*, Prism, Sydney, 1975.
—— 'The Garden and the City', *Westerly*, vol. 27, no. 4, December 1982, pp. 99–104.

Hughes, Robert, *The Fatal Shore*, Alfred A. Knopf, 1986. Reprint Random House, Sydney, 2009.

Jolley, Elizabeth, 'A Sort of Gift: Images of Perth', in Drusilla Modjeska (ed.), *Inner Cities: Australian Women's Memory of Place*, Penguin, Ringwood, 1989.

Jones, Gail, *Black Mirror*, Picador, Sydney, 2002.

Kinnane, Stephen, *Shadow Lines*, Fremantle Arts Centre Press, Fremantle, 2003.

Kinsella, John & Lucy, Niall, *The Ballad of Moondyne Joe*, Fremantle Press, Fremantle, 2012.

Laurence, John, 'Claude de Bernales, the promoter', in Lyall Hunt (ed.), *Westralian Portraits*, University of Western Australia Press, Crawley, 1979.

Mackenzie, Kenneth Seaforth, *The Young Desire It*, Jonathan Cape, London, 1937. Reprint Angus & Robertson, Sydney, 1972.

Marshall, Debi, *The Devil's Garden: The Claremont Serial Killings*, Random House, Sydney, 2007.

Moore, George Fletcher, *Diary of Ten Years*, University of Western Australia Press, Crawley, 1978.

Prichard, Katharine Susannah, *Intimate Strangers*, Jonathan Cape, London, 1937.

Reid, Mark, *Parochial*, Fremantle Arts Centre Press, 2000.

Roberts, Jane, *Two Years at Sea: Being the Narrative of a Voyage to the Swan River and Van Dieman's Land, During the Years 1829, 30, 31*, British Library, Historical Print Editions, 2011.

Seddon, George, *Sense of Place*, University of Western Australia Press, Crawley, 1972.

—— *Swan Song: Reflections on Perth and Western Australia 1956–1995*, Centre for Studies in Western Australian Literature, Crawley, 1995.

Tan, Shaun, *Suburban Odyssey*, Fremantle Arts Centre, Fremantle, 2012.

Vinciguerra, Guy, *Crossing the Line*, Parallax, Tuart Hill, 2001.

Walker, Brenda, *The Wing of Night*, Penguin, Camberwell, 2005.

Walsh, M., *Mother of the Gumnuts: Her Life and Work*, Angus & Robertson, Sydney, 1985, as quoted in *Swan Song: Reflections on Perth and Western Australia 1956–1995*, Centre for Studies in Western Australian Literature, Crawley, 1995.

Waten, Judah, *Alien Son*, Lloyd O'Neill, Hawthorn, 1974.

Weller, Richard, *Boomtown 2050: Scenarios for a Rapidly Growing City*, University of Western Australia Press, Crawley, 2009.

White, Kate, 'Bessie Rischbieth, the feminist', in Lyall Hunt (ed.) *Westralian Portraits*, University of Western Australia Press, Crawley, 1979.

White, Terri-ann, *Finding Theodore and Brina*, Fremantle Arts Centre Press, Fremantle, 2001.

Wilson, Josephine, *Cusp*, University of Western Australia Press, Crawley, 2005.

Winton, Tim, *Cloudstreet*, Penguin, Ringwood, 1992.

—— *Land's Edge*, Pan Macmillan, Sydney, 1993.

Bibliography

'Mug's Game' by Dave Warner's From the Suburbs, written by David Warner (Mushroom Music Publishing). Reprinted with permission.

'Spanish Blue' by The Triffids, written by David McComb (Mushroom Music Publishing). Reprinted with permission.

'The end of an era: Power Station put on standby', *Fremantle Gazette*, 16 July 1985, p. 10.